FOREWORD

The collection of "Everything Will Be Okay" travel phrasebooks published by T&P Books is designed for people traveling abroad for tourism and business. The phrasebooks contain what matters most - the essentials for basic communication. This is an indispensable set of phrases to "survive" while abroad.

This phrasebook will help you in most cases where you need to ask something, get directions, find out how much something costs, etc. It can also resolve difficult communication situations where gestures just won't help.

This book contains a lot of phrases that have been grouped according to the most relevant topics. The edition also includes a small vocabulary that contains roughly 3,000 of the most frequently used words. Another section of the phrasebook provides a gastronomical dictionary that may help you order food at a restaurant or buy groceries at the store.

Take "Everything Will Be Okay" phrasebook with you on the road and you'll have an irreplaceable traveling companion who will help you find your way out of any situation and teach you to not fear speaking with foreigners.

TABLE OF CONTENTS

T&P Books Publishing

Travel phrasebooks collection
«Everything Will Be Okay!»

T&P Books Publishing

PHRASEBOOK

— KYRGYZ —

By Andrey Taranov

THE MOST IMPORTANT PHRASES

This phrasebook contains the most important phrases and questions for basic communication
Everything you need to survive overseas

T&P BOOKS

Phrasebook + 3000-word dictionary

English-Kyrgyz phrasebook & topical vocabulary

By Andrey Taranov

The collection of "Everything Will Be Okay" travel phrasebooks published by T&P Books is designed for people traveling abroad for tourism and business. The phrasebooks contain what matters most - the essentials for basic communication. This is an indispensable set of phrases to "survive" while abroad.

This book also includes a small topical vocabulary that contains roughly 3,000 of the most frequently used words. Another section of the phrasebook provides a gastronomical dictionary that may help you order food at a restaurant or buy groceries at the store.

T&P Books Publishing
www.tpbooks.com

ISBN: 978-1-78767-151-5

This book is also available in E-book formats.
Please visit www.tpbooks.com or the major online bookstores.

PRONUNCIATION

T&P phonetic alphabet	Kyrgyz example	English example
[a]	манжа [mandʒa]	shorter than in ask
[e]	келечек [keletʃek]	elm, medal
[i]	жигит [dʒigit]	shorter than in feet
[ɪ]	кубаныч [kubanɪtʃ]	big, America
[o]	мактоо [maktoo]	pod, John
[u]	узундук [uzunduk]	book
[ʉ]	алюминий [alʉminij]	youth, usually
[y]	түнкү [tynky]	fuel, tuna
[b]	ашкабак [aʃkabak]	baby, book
[d]	адам [adam]	day, doctor
[dʒ]	жыгач [dʒɪgatʃ]	joke, general
[f]	флейта [flejta]	face, food
[g]	тегерек [tegerek]	game, gold
[j]	бейрөк [bøjrøk]	yes, New York
[k]	карапа [karapa]	clock, kiss
[l]	алтын [altɪn]	lace, people
[m]	бешмант [beʃmant]	magic, milk
[n]	найза [najza]	name, normal
[ŋ]	булуң [buluŋ]	ring
[p]	пайдубал [pajdubal]	pencil, private
[r]	рахмат [raχmat]	rice, radio
[s]	сагызган [sagɪzgan]	city, boss
[ʃ]	бурулуш [buruluʃ]	machine, shark
[t]	түтүн [tytyn]	tourist, trip
[χ]	пахтадан [paχtadan]	hot, hobby
[ts]	шприц [ʃprits]	cats, tsetse fly
[tʃ]	биринчи [birintʃi]	church, French
[v]	квартал [kvartal]	very, river
[z]	казуу [kazuu]	zebra, please
[ʲ]	руль, актёр [rulʲ, aktʲor]	palatalization sign

LIST OF ABBREVIATIONS

English abbreviations

ab.	-	about
adj	-	adjective
adv	-	adverb
anim.	-	animate
as adj	-	attributive noun used as adjective
e.g.	-	for example
etc.	-	et cetera
fam.	-	familiar
fem.	-	feminine
form.	-	formal
inanim.	-	inanimate
masc.	-	masculine
math	-	mathematics
mil.	-	military
n	-	noun
pl	-	plural
pron.	-	pronoun
sb	-	somebody
sing.	-	singular
sth	-	something
v aux	-	auxiliary verb
vi	-	intransitive verb
vi, vt	-	intransitive, transitive verb
vt	-	transitive verb

T&P BOOKS

KYRGYZ PHRASEBOOK

This section contains
important phrases that may
come in handy in various
real-life situations.
The phrasebook will help
you ask for directions, clarify
a price, buy tickets, and
order food at a restaurant

T&P Books Publishing

PHRASEBOOK CONTENTS

T&P Books Publishing

The bare minimum

Excuse me, ...	**Кечиресиз, ...** ketʃiresiz, ...
Hello.	**Саламатсызбы.** salamatsızbı.
Thank you.	**Рахмат.** raχmat.
Good bye.	**Көрүшкөнчө.** køryʃkønʧø.
Yes.	**Ооба.** ooba.
No.	**Жок.** dʒok.
I don't know.	**Мен билбейм.** men bilbejm.
Where? | Where to? | When?	**Каякта? | Каякка? | Качан?** kajakta? | kajakka? | katʃan?

I need ...	**Мага ... керек эле.** maga ... kerek ele.
I want ...	**Мен ... гым келет.** men ... gım kelet.
Do you have ...?	**Силерде ... барбы?** silerde ... barbı?
Is there a ... here?	**Бул жерде ... барбы?** bul dʒerde ... barbı?
May I ...?	**Мага ... болобу?** maga ... bolobu?
..., please (polite request)	**Сураныч** suranıʧ

I'm looking for ...	**Мен ... издеп жаттым эле.** men ... izdep dʒattım ele.
the restroom	**даараткана** daaratkana
an ATM	**банкомат** bankomat
a pharmacy (drugstore)	**дарыкана** darıkana
a hospital	**оорукана** oorukana
the police station	**милиция бөлүмү** militsija bølymy
the subway	**метро** metro

a taxi	**такси** taksi
the train station	**вокзал** vokzal

My name is …	**Менин атым …** menin atım …
What's your name?	**Сиздин атыңыз ким?** sizdin atıŋız kim?
Could you please help me?	**Мага жардам берип коюңузчу.** maga dʒardam berip kodʒuŋuztʃu.
I've got a problem.	**Менде көйгөй чыкты.** mende køygøj tʃıktı.
I don't feel well.	**Мен өзүмдү жаман сезип жатам.** men øzymdy dʒaman sezip dʒatam.
Call an ambulance!	**Тез жардамды чакырып коюңузчу!** tez dʒardamdı tʃakırıp kodʒuŋuztʃu!
May I make a call?	**Телефон чалып алсам болобу?** telefon tʃalıp alsam bolobu?

I'm sorry.	**Кечирип коюңуз** ketʃirip kojuŋuz
You're welcome.	**Эчтеке эмес** etʃteke emes

I, me	**мен** men
you (inform.)	**сен** sen
he	**ал** al
she	**ал** al
they (masc.)	**алар** alar
they (fem.)	**алар** alar
we	**биз** biz
you (pl)	**сиз** siz
you (sg, form.)	**Сиз** siz

ENTRANCE	**КИРҮҮ** kiryy
EXIT	**ЧЫГУУ** tʃıguu
OUT OF ORDER	**ИШТЕБЕЙТ** iʃtebejt
CLOSED	**ЖАБЫК** dʒabık

OPEN	**АЧЫК** atʃık
FOR WOMEN	**АЙЫМДАР ҮЧҮН** ajımdar ytʃyn
FOR MEN	**ЭРКЕКТЕР ҮЧҮН** erkekter ytʃyn

Questions

Where?	**Каякта?** kajakta?
Where to?	**Кайда?** kajda?
Where from?	**Каяктан?** kajaktan?
Why?	**Эмне үчүн?** emne ytʃyn?
For what reason?	**Эмнеге?** emnege?
When?	**Качан?** katʃan?
How long?	**Канчага?** kantʃaga?
At what time?	**Саат канчада?** saat kantʃada?
How much?	**Канча турат?** kantʃa turat?
Do you have ...?	**Силерде ... барбы?** silerde ... barbɪ?
Where is ...?	**... каякта жайгашкан?** ... kajakta dʒajgaʃkan?
What time is it?	**Саат канча болду?** saat kantʃa boldu?
May I make a call?	**Телефон чалып алсам болобу?** telefon tʃalɪp alsam bolobu?
Who's there?	**Ким бул?** kim bul?
Can I smoke here?	**Бул жерде тамеки чексем болобу?** bul dʒerde tameki tʃeksem bolobu?
May I ...?	**Мага ... болобу?** maga ... bolobu?

Needs

I'd like …	**Мен … дедим эле.** men … dedim ele.
I don't want …	**Мен … келген жок.** men … kelgen dʒok.
I'm thirsty.	**Мен ичким келет.** men itʃkim kelet.
I want to sleep.	**Мен уйкум келет.** men ujkum kelet.

I want …	**Мен …** men …
to wash up	**жуунуп алайын дедим эле** dʒuunup alajın dedim ele
to brush my teeth	**тишимди тазалап алайын дедим эле** tiʃimdi tazalap alajın dedim ele
to rest a while	**бир аз эс алгым келип жатат** bir az es algım kelip dʒatat
to change my clothes	**кийимимди которуп алайын дедим эле** kijimimdi kotorup alajın dedim ele
to go back to the hotel	**мейманканага кайра кетким келет** mejmankanaga kajra ketkim kelet
to buy …	**… сатып алгым келет** … satıp algım kelet
to go to …	**… барып келгим келет** … barıp kelgim kelet
to visit …	**… көрүп келсемби дейм** … kørjp kelsembi dejm
to meet with …	**… менен жолугайын дейм** … menen dʒolugajın dejm
to make a call	**чалайын дейм** tʃalajın dejm

I'm tired.	**Мен чарчадым.** men tʃartʃadım.
We are tired.	**Биз чарчадык.** biz tʃartʃadık.
I'm cold.	**Мен үшүп кеттим.** men yʃyp kettim.
I'm hot.	**Мен ысып кеттим.** men ısıp kettim.
I'm OK.	**Баары жакшы.** baarı dʒakʃı.

I need to make a call.

Мен чалышым керек.
men tʃalıʃım kerek.

I need to go to the restroom.

Мен дааратканага барышым керек.
men daaratkanaga barıʃim kerek.

I have to go.

Мен кетишим керек.
men ketiʃim kerek.

I have to go now.

Мен азыр кетишим керек.
men azır ketiʃim kerek.

Asking for directions

Excuse me, ...	**Кечиресиз, ...** ketʃiresiz, ...
Where is ...?	**... каякта жайгашкан?** ... kajakta dʒajgaʃkan?
Which way is ...?	**... кайсы жакта жайгашканын билбейсизби?** ... kajsı dʒakta dʒajgaʃkanın bilbejsizbi?
Could you help me, please?	**Мага жардам берип коюңузчу.** maga dʒardam berip kodʒuŋuztʃu.

I'm looking for ...	**Мен ... издеп жаттым эле.** men ... izdep dʒattım ele.
I'm looking for the exit.	**Каяктан чыксам болот?** kajaktan tʃıksam bolot?
I'm going to ...	**Мен ... кетип баратам.** men ... ketip baratam.
Am I going the right way to ...?	**... жакка туура баратамбы?** ... dʒakka tuura baratambı?

Is it far?	**Бул жерден алыспы?** bul dʒerden alıspı?
Can I get there on foot?	**Мен ал жакка жөө жете аламбы?** men al dʒakka dʒøø dʒete alambı?
Can you show me on the map?	**Ал жакты картадан көрсөтүп бериңизчи.** al dʒaktı kartadan kørsøtyp beriŋiztʃi.
Show me where we are right now.	**Биз азыр кайсы жерде турабыз, көрсөтүп бериңизчи.** biz azır kajsı dʒerde turabız, kørsøtyp beriŋiztʃi.

Here	**Бул жерде** bul dʒerde
There	**Тээтиги жерде** teetigi dʒerde
This way	**Бул жак менен** bul dʒak menen

Turn right.	**Азыр оңго.** azır oŋgo.
Turn left.	**Азыр солго.** azır solgo.

first (second, third) turn

биринчи (экинчи, үчүнчү) бурулуш
birintʃi (ekintʃi, ytʃyntʃy) buruluʃ

to the right

оңго
oŋgo

to the left

солго
solgo

Go straight ahead.

Түз барыңыз.
tyz barıŋız.

Signs

WELCOME!	**КОШ КЕЛИҢИЗДЕР!** koʃ keliŋizder!
ENTRANCE	**КИРҮҮ** kiryy
EXIT	**ЧЫГУУ** ʧɩguu

PUSH	**ТҮРТҮҢҮЗ** tyrtyŋyz
PULL	**ТАРТЫҢЫЗ** tartɩŋɩz
OPEN	**АЧЫК** aʧɩk
CLOSED	**ЖАБЫК** ʤabɩk

FOR WOMEN	**АЙЫМДАР ҮЧҮН** ajɩmdar yʧyn
FOR MEN	**ЭРКЕКТЕР ҮЧҮН** erkekter yʧyn
GENTLEMEN, GENTS	**ЭРКЕКТЕР ДААРАТКАНАСЫ** erkekter daaratkanasɩ
WOMEN	**АЙЫМДАР ДААРАТКАНАСЫ** ajɩmdar daaratkanasɩ

DISCOUNTS	**АРЗАНДАТУУЛАР** arzandatuular
SALE	**САТЫП ТҮГӨТҮҮ** satɩp tygøtyy
FREE	**БЕКЕР** beker
NEW!	**СААМАЛЫК!** saamalɩk!
ATTENTION!	**КӨҢҮЛ БУРУҢУЗ!** køŋyl buruŋuz!

NO VACANCIES	**ОРУН ЖОК** orun ʤok
RESERVED	**КАМДЫК БУЙРУТМАЛАГАН** kamdɩk bujrutmalagan
ADMINISTRATION	**АДМИНИСТРАЦИЯ** administratsija
STAFF ONLY	**ЖААМАТ ҮЧҮН ГАНА** ʤaamat yʧyn gana

BEWARE OF THE DOG!

КАБАНААК ИТ
kabanaak it

NO SMOKING!

ТАМЕКИ ЧЕГҮҮГӨ БОЛБОЙТ!
tameki ʧegyygø bolbojt!

DO NOT TOUCH!

КОЛУҢАР МЕНЕН КАРМАБАГЫЛА!
koluŋar menen karmabagıla!

DANGEROUS

КОРКУНУЧ БАР
korkunuʧ bar

DANGER

КОРКУНУЧТУУ
korkunuʧtuu

HIGH VOLTAGE

ЖОГОРКУ ЧЫҢАЛУУ
dʒogorku ʧiŋaluu

NO SWIMMING!

СУУГА ТҮШҮҮГӨ БОЛБОЙТ
suuga tyʃyygø bolbojt

OUT OF ORDER

ИШТЕБЕЙТ
iʃtebejt

FLAMMABLE

ӨРТ ЧЫГУУ КОРКУНУЧУ
ørt ʧiguu korkunuʧu

FORBIDDEN

БОЛБОЙТ
bolbojt

NO TRESPASSING!

ӨТҮҮГӨ БОЛБОЙТ
øtyygø bolbojt

WET PAINT

СЫРДАЛГАН
sırdalgan

CLOSED FOR RENOVATIONS

ОҢДОО ИШТЕРИ ҮЧҮН ЖАБЫК
ondoo iʃteri yʧyn dʒabık

WORKS AHEAD

ЖОЛ ОҢДОО ИШТЕРИ
dʒol oŋdoo iʃteri

DETOUR

АЙЛАНЫП ӨТМӨ ЖОЛ
ajlanıp øtmø dʒol

Transportation. General phrases

plane	**самолёт** samolʲot
train	**поезд** poezd
bus	**автобус** avtobus
ferry	**паром** parom
taxi	**такси** taksi
car	**машина** maʃina

schedule	**ырааттама** ıraattama
Where can I see the schedule?	**Ырааттаманы кайсыл жерден көрсөм болот?** iraattamanı kajsıl dʒerden kørsøm bolot?
workdays (weekdays)	**иш күндөрү** iʃ kyndøry
weekends	**эс алуу күндөрү** es aluu kyndøry
holidays	**майрам күндөрү** majram kyndøry

DEPARTURE	**ЖӨНӨӨ** dʒønøø
ARRIVAL	**КЕЛҮҮ** kelyy
DELAYED	**КАРМАЛУУ** karmaluu
CANCELLED	**ЖОККО ЧЫГАРЫЛГАН** dʒokko tʃıgarilgan

next (train, etc.)	**кийинки** kijinki
first	**биринчи** birintʃi
last	**акыркы** akırkı

When is the next ...?

Кийинки ... качан келет?
kijinki ... katʃan kelet?

When is the first ...?

Биринчи ... качан кетет?
birintʃi ... katʃan ketet?

When is the last ...?

Акыркы ... качан кетет?
akırkı ... katʃan ketet?

transfer (change of trains, etc.)

которулуп түшүү
kotorulup tyʃyy

to make a transfer

которулуп түшүү
kotorulup tyʃyy

Do I need to make a transfer?

Которулуп түшүшүм керекпи?
kotorulup tyʃyʃym kerekpi?

Buying tickets

Where can I buy tickets?	**Билетти каяктан сатып алсам болот.** biletti kajaktan satıp alsam bolot.
ticket	**билет** bilet
to buy a ticket	**билетти сатып алуу** biletti satıp aluu
ticket price	**билеттин баасы** bilettin baası

Where to?	**Кайда?** kajda?
To what station?	**Кайсы станцияга чейин?** kajsı stantsijaga tʃejin?
I need …	**Мага … керек.** maga … kerek.
one ticket	**бир билет** bir bilet
two tickets	**эки билет** eki bilet
three tickets	**үч билет** ytʃ bilet
one-way	**бир тарапка** bir tarapka
round-trip	**барып келүү** barıp kelyy
first class	**биринчи класс** birintʃi klass
second class	**экинчи класс** ekintʃi klass

today	**бүгүн** bygyn
tomorrow	**эртең** erteŋ
the day after tomorrow	**бүрсүгүнү** byrsygyny
in the morning	**эртең менен** erteŋ menen
in the afternoon	**күндүз** kyndyz
in the evening	**кечинде** ketʃinde

aisle seat

кире бериш жактагы орун
kire beriʃ dʒaktagı orun

window seat

терезе жанындагы орун
tereze dʒanındagı orun

How much?

Канча турат?
kantʃa turat?

Can I pay by credit card?

Карточка менен төлөсөм болобу?
kartotʃka menen tøløsøm bolobu?

Bus

bus	**автобус** avtobus
intercity bus	**шаар аралык автобус** ʃaar aralık avtobus
bus stop	**автобус аялдамасы** avtobus ajaldaması
Where's the nearest bus stop?	**Жакын арада автобустун аялдамасы барбы?** dʒakın arada avtobustun ajaldaması barbı?
number (bus ~, etc.)	**номер** nomer
Which bus do I take to get to …?	**Кайсы автобус … чейин барат?** kajsı avtobus … tʃejin barat?
Does this bus go to …?	**Бул автобус … чейин барабы?** bul avtobus … tʃejin barabı?
How frequent are the buses?	**Автобустар канчалык тез жүрүп турат?** avtobustar kantʃalık tez dʒyryp turat?

every 15 minutes	**он беш мүнөт сайын** on beʃ mynøt sajın
every half hour	**ар жарым саат сайын** ar dʒarım saat sajın
every hour	**ар бир саатта** ar bir saatta
several times a day	**бир күндө бир нече жолу** bir kyndø bir netʃe dʒolu
… times a day	**бир күндө … жолу** bir kyndø … dʒolu

schedule	**ырааттама** ıraattama
Where can I see the schedule?	**Ырааттаманы кайсыл жерден көрсөм болот?** iraattamanı kajsıl dʒerden kørsøm bolot?
When is the next bus?	**Кийинки автобус качан келет?** kijinki avtobus katʃan kelet?
When is the first bus?	**Биринчи автобус качан кетет?** birintʃi avtobus katʃan ketet?
When is the last bus?	**Акыркы автобус качан кетет?** akırkı avtobus katʃan ketet?

stop

аялдама
ajaldama

next stop

кийинки аялдама
kijinki ajaldama

last stop (terminus)

акыркы аялдама
akırkı ajaldama

Stop here, please.

Ушул жерден токтотуп койсоңуз.
uʃul dʒerden toktotup kojsoŋuz.

Excuse me, this is my stop.

Бул аялдамадан токтотуп коёсузбу?
bul ajaldamadan toktotup kojosuzbu?

Train

train	**поезд** poezd
suburban train	**шаардан тышкары барчу поезд** ʃaardan tıʃkarı bartʃu poezd
long-distance train	**алыс аралыкка журүүчу поезд** alıs aralıkka dʒyryytʃy poezd
train station	**вокзал** vokzal
Excuse me, where is the exit to the platform?	**Кечиресиз, поезддер жакка кантип барсам болот?** ketʃiresiz, poezdder dʒakka kantip barsam bolot?

Does this train go to …?	**Бул поезд … чейин барабы?** bul poezd … tʃejin barabı?
next train	**кийинки поезд** kijinki poezd
When is the next train?	**Кийинки поезд качан келет?** kijinki poezd katʃan kelet?
Where can I see the schedule?	**Ырааттаманы кайсыл жерден көрсөм болот?** iraattamanı kajsıl dʒerden kørsøm bolot?
From which platform?	**Кайсы платформадан?** kajsı platformadan?
When does the train arrive in …?	**Поезд … качан келет?** poezd … katʃan kelet?

Please help me.	**Мага жардам берип коюңузчу.** maga dʒardam berip kodʒuŋuztʃu.

I'm looking for my seat.	**Мен өз ордумду издеп жаттым эле.** men øz ordumdu izdep dʒattım ele.
We're looking for our seats.	**Биз өз ордубузду издеп жатабыз.** biz øz ordubuzdu izdep dʒatabız.
My seat is taken.	**Менин ордум бош эмес.** menin ordum boʃ emes.
Our seats are taken.	**Биздин орундарыбыз бош эмес.** bizdin orundarıbız boʃ emes.
I'm sorry but this is my seat.	**Кечиресиз, бирок бул менин орунум.** ketʃiresiz, birok bul menin orunum.

Is this seat taken?

Бул орун бошпу?
bul orun boʃpu?

May I sit here?

Мен бул жерге отурсам болобу?
men bul ʤerge otursam bolobu?

On the train. Dialogue (No ticket)

Ticket, please.
Билетиңизди көрсөтүп коюңузчу.
biletiŋizdi kørsøtyp kojɥŋuzʧu.

I don't have a ticket.
Менин билетим жок.
menin biletim ʤok.

I lost my ticket.
Мен билетимди жоготуп алдым.
men biletimdi ʤogotup aldım.

I forgot my ticket at home.
Мен билетимди үйгө унутуп коюптурмун.
men biletimdi yjgø unutup kojɥpturmun.

You can buy a ticket from me.
Сиз билетти менден сатып алсаңыз болот.
siz biletti menden satıp alsaŋız bolot.

You will also have to pay a fine.
Сиз дагы айып төлөшүңүз керек.
siz dagı ajıp tøløʃyŋyz kerek.

Okay.
Макул.
makul.

Where are you going?
Сиз каякка баратасыз?
siz kajakka baratasız?

I'm going to ...
... чейин барам.
... ʧejin baram.

How much? I don't understand.
Канча турат? Түшүнбөй жатам.
kanʧa turat? tyʃynbøj ʤatam.

Write it down, please.
Жазып бериңизчи.
ʤazıp beriŋizʧi.

Okay. Can I pay with a credit card?
Макул. Мен карточка менен төлөсөм болобу?
makul. men kartoʧka menen tøløsøm bolobu?

Yes, you can.
Ооба, болот.
ooba, bolot.

Here's your receipt.
Мына сиздин эсеп дүмүрчөгү.
mına sizdin esep dymyrʧøgy.

Sorry about the fine.
Айып төлөгөнүңүз үчүн кечирим сурайм.
ajıp tøløgønyŋyz yʧyn keʧirim surajm.

That's okay. It was my fault.

Эч нерсе эмес. Мен өзүм күнөөлүмүн.
etʃ nerse emes. men øzym kynøølymyn.

Enjoy your trip.

Жолуңуз шыдыр болсун.
dʒoluŋuz ʃıdır bolsun.

Taxi

taxi	**такси** taksi
taxi driver	**таксист** taksist
to catch a taxi	**такси кармоо** taksi karmoo
taxi stand	**Такси токтоочу жай** taksi toktootʃu dʒaj
Where can I get a taxi?	**Таксини каяктан кармасам болот?** taksini kajaktan karmasam bolot?
to call a taxi	**такси чакыруу** taksi tʃakıruu
I need a taxi.	**Мага такси керек болуп жатат.** maga taksi kerek bolup dʒatat.
Right now.	**Азыр, тез арада.** azır, tez arada.
What is your address (location)?	**Сиздин дарегиңиз?** sizdin dareginiz?
My address is …	**Менин дарегим …** menin daregim …
Your destination?	**Сиз каякка барасыз?** siz kajakka barasız?
Excuse me, …	**Кечиресиз, …** ketʃiresiz, …
Are you available?	**Сиз бошсузбу?** siz boʃsuzbu?
How much is it to get to …?	**… чейин канча болот?** … tʃejin kantʃa bolot?
Do you know where it is?	**Ал жак каякта экенин сиз билесизби?** al dʒak kajakta ekenin siz bilesizbi?
Airport, please.	**Аэропортко жеткирип койсоңуз.** aeroportko dʒetkirip kojsoŋuz.
Stop here, please.	**Бул жерден токтотуп койсоңуз.** bul dʒerden toktotup kojsoŋuz.
It's not here.	**Бул жерде эмес.** bul dʒerde emes.
This is the wrong address.	**Бул туура эмес дарек.** bul tuura emes darek.

Turn left.	**Азыр солго.** azır solgo.
Turn right.	**Азыр оңго.** azır oŋgo.

How much do I owe you?	**Сизге канча төлөйм?** sizge kanʧa tøløjm?
I'd like a receipt, please.	**Мага чек берип коюңузчу.** maga ʧek berip kojuŋuzʧu.
Keep the change.	**Ашкан акчаны жөн эле коюңуз.** aʃkan akʧanı dʒøn ele kodʒuŋuz.

Would you please wait for me?	**Мени күтүп туруңузчу.** meni kytyp turuŋuzʧu.
five minutes	**беш мүнөт** beʃ mynøt
ten minutes	**он мүнөт** on mynøt
fifteen minutes	**он беш мүнөт** on beʃ mynøt
twenty minutes	**жыйырма мүнөт** dʒıjırma mynøt
half an hour	**жарым саат** dʒarım saat

Hotel

Hello.	**Саламатсызбы.** salamatsızbı.
My name is …	**Менин атым …** menin atım …
I have a reservation.	**Мен бөлмөгө камдык буйрутма жасадым эле.** men bølmøgø kamdık bujrutma dʒasadım ele.

I need …	**Мага … керек эле.** maga … kerek ele.
a single room	**бир орундуу бөлмө** bir orunduu bølmø
a double room	**эки орундуу бөлмө** eki orunduu bølmø
How much is that?	**Ал канча турат?** al kantʃa turat?
That's a bit expensive.	**Бул бир аз кымбатыраак болуп калат.** bul bir az kımbatıraak bolup kalat.

Do you have anything else?	**Силерде дагы башка бөлмөлөр барбы?** silerde dagı baʃka bølmølør barbı?
I'll take it.	**Мен ошону алам.** men oʃonu alam.
I'll pay in cash.	**Мен накталай төлөйм.** men naktalaj tøløjm.

I've got a problem.	**Менде көйгөй чыкты.** mende køygøj tʃıktı.
My … is broken.	**Менин … бузук экен.** menin … buzuk eken.
My … is out of order.	**Менин … иштебей жатат.** menin … iʃtebej dʒatat.
TV	**сыналгым** sınalgım
air conditioner	**аба салкындаткычым** aba salkındatkıtʃım
tap	**краным** kranım

shower	**душум**
	duʃum
sink	**раковинам**
	rakovinam
safe	**сейфим**
	sejfim
door lock	**кулпум**
	kulpum
electrical outlet	**розеткам**
	rozetkam
hairdryer	**чач кургаткычым**
	tʃatʃ kurgatkɪtʃɪm

I don't have …	**Менин … жок.**
	menin … dʒok.
water	**суу**
	suu
light	**жарык**
	dʒarɪk
electricity	**электр кубаты**
	elektr kubatɪ

Can you give me …?	**Мага … берип коесузбу?**
	maga … berip koesuzbu?
a towel	**сүлгү**
	sylgy
a blanket	**жууркан**
	dʒuurkan
slippers	**тапичке**
	tapitʃke
a robe	**халат**
	χalat
shampoo	**шампунь**
	ʃampunʲ
soap	**самын**
	samɪn

I'd like to change rooms.	**Мен бөлмөмдү алмаштырайын дедим эле.**
	men bølmømdy almaʃtɪrajɪn dedim ele.
I can't find my key.	**Мен ачкычымды таппай жатам.**
	men atʃkɪtʃɪmdɪ tappaj dʒatam.
Could you open my room, please?	**Менин бөлмөмдү ачып берип коюңузчу.**
	menin bølmømdy atʃɪp berip kojɯŋuztʃu.
Who's there?	**Ким бул?**
	kim bul?
Come in!	**Кире бериңиз!**
	kire beriŋiz!

Just a minute!	**Бир мүнөт!** bir mynøt!
Not right now, please.	**Кечиресиз, азыр эмес.** ketʃiresiz, azır emes.

Come to my room, please.	**Мага кирип койгулачы.** maga kirip kojgulatʃı.
I'd like to order food service.	**Мен тамакты бөлмөгө заказ кылайын дегем.** men tamaktı bølmøgø zakaz kılajın degem.
My room number is ...	**Менин бөлмөмдүн номери ...** menin bølmømdyn nomeri ...

I'm leaving ...	**Мен ... кеткени жатам.** men ... ketkeni dʒatam.
We're leaving ...	**Биз ... кеткени жатабыз.** biz ... ketkeni dʒatabız.
right now	**азыр** azır
this afternoon	**бүгүн түштөн кийин** bygyn tyʃtøn kijin
tonight	**бүгүн кечинде** bygyn ketʃinde
tomorrow	**эртең** erteŋ
tomorrow morning	**эртең эртең менен** erteŋ erteŋ menen
tomorrow evening	**эртең кечинде** erteŋ ketʃinde
the day after tomorrow	**бүрсүгүнү** byrsygyny

I'd like to pay.	**Мен эсептешип коеюн дегем.** men ese`pteʃip koejun degem.
Everything was wonderful.	**Баары жакшы болду.** baarı dʒakʃı boldu.
Where can I get a taxi?	**Таксини каяктан кармасам болот?** taksini kajaktan karmasam bolot?
Would you call a taxi for me, please?	**Мага такси чакырып коюңузчу.** maga taksi tʃakırıp kojuŋuztʃu.

Restaurant

Can I look at the menu, please?	**Силердин менюнерди көрсөм болобу?** silerdin menuŋerdi kørsøm bolobu?
Table for one.	**Бир кишилик стол керек.** bir kiʃilik stol kerek.
There are two (three, four) of us.	**Биз экөөбүз (үчөөбүз, төртөөбүз).** biz ekøøbyz (yʧøøbyz, tørtøøbyz).

Smoking	**Тамеки чеккендер үчүн** tameki ʧekkender yʧyn
No smoking	**Чекпегендер үчүн** ʧekpegender yʧyn
Excuse me! (addressing a waiter)	**Кичипейилдикке!** kiʧipejildikke!
menu	**меню** menu
wine list	**шараптардын картасы** ʃaraptardın kartası
The menu, please.	**Менюну берип коюнузчу.** menunu berip kojuŋuzʧu.

Are you ready to order?	**Буйрутма бергенге даярсызбы?** bujrutma bergenge dajarsızbı?
What will you have?	**Буйрутманыз эмне болот?** bujrutmaŋız emne bolot?
I'll have …	**Мен … алам** men … alam

I'm a vegetarian.	**Мен эт жебейм.** men et dʒebejm.
meat	**эт** et
fish	**балык** balık
vegetables	**жемиштер** dʒemiʃter
Do you have vegetarian dishes?	**Силерде эт кошулбаган тамактары барбы?** silerde et koʃulbagan tamaktarı barbı?
I don't eat pork.	**Мен чочконун этин жебейм.** men ʧoʧkonun etin dʒebejm.

Band-Aid	**Ал эт жебейт.** al et dʒebejt.
I am allergic to …	**Менин … аллергиям бар.** menin … allergijam bar.

Would you please bring me …	**Мага … алып келип бериңизчи.** maga … alıp kelip beriŋiztʃi.
salt | pepper | sugar	**туз | калемпир | кумшекер** tuz | kalempir | kumʃeker
coffee | tea | dessert	**кофе | чай | десерт** kofe | tʃaj | desert
water | sparkling | plain	**суу | газы менен | газы жок** suu | gazı menen | gazı dʒok
a spoon | fork | knife	**кашык | вилка | бычак** kaʃık | vilka | bıtʃak
a plate | napkin	**табак | салфетка** tabak | salfetka

Enjoy your meal!	**Тамагыңыз таттуу болсун!** tamagıŋız tattuu bolsun!
One more, please.	**Дагы алып келип бериңизчи.** dagı alıp kelip beriŋiztʃi.
It was very delicious.	**Аябай даамдуу болуптур.** ajabaj daamduu boluptur.

check | change | tip	**эсеп | ашкан акча | чайга** esep | aʃkan aktʃa | tʃajga
Check, please. (Could I have the check, please?)	**Эсептеп коюңузчу.** eseptep kojuŋuztʃu.
Can I pay by credit card?	**Карточка менен төлөсөм болобу?** kartotʃka menen tøløsøm bolobu?
I'm sorry, there's a mistake here.	**Кечиресиз, бул жакта ката кетип калыптыр.** ketʃiresiz, bul dʒakta kata ketip kalıptır.

Shopping

Can I help you?
Сизге жардам берсем болобу?
sizge dʒardam bersem bolobu?

Do you have ...?
Силерде ... барбы?
silerde ... barbı?

I'm looking for ...
Мен ... издеп жаттым эле.
men ... izdep dʒattım ele.

I need ...
Мага ... керек эле.
maga ... kerek ele.

I'm just looking.
Мен жөн гана көрүп жатам.
men dʒøn gana køryp dʒatam.

We're just looking.
Биз жөн гана көрүп жатабыз.
biz dʒøn gana køryp dʒatabız.

I'll come back later.
Мен ананыраак келем.
men ananıraak kelem.

We'll come back later.
Биз ананыраак келебиз.
biz ananıraak kelebiz.

discounts | sale
арзандатуулар | сатып түгөтүү
arzandatuular | satıp tygøtyy

Would you please show me ...
Мага ... көрсөтүп коюңузчу.
maga ... kørsøtyp kojuŋuztʃu.

Would you please give me ...
Мага ... берип коюңузчу.
maga ... berip kojuŋuztʃu.

Can I try it on?
Мен кийип көрсөм болобу?
men kijip kørsøm bolobu?

Excuse me, where's the fitting room?
Каяктан кийип көрсөм болот?
kajaktan kijip kørsøm bolot?

Which color would you like?
Кайсыл өңүн каалап жатасыз?
kajsıl øŋyn kaalap dʒatasız?

size | length
өлчөм | бой
øltʃøm | boj

How does it fit?
Чак келдиби?
tʃak keldibi?

How much is it?
Бул канча турат?
bul kantʃa turat?

That's too expensive.
Бул аябай кымбат.
bul ajabaj kımbat.

I'll take it.
Мен муну сатып алам.
men munu satıp alam.

Excuse me, where do I pay?
Кечиресиз, касса кайсы жакта?
ketʃiresiz, kassa kajsı dʒakta?

Will you pay in cash or credit card?

Кандай төлөсүз? Накталайбы же карточка мененби?
kandaj tøløsyz? naktalajbı ʤe kartotʃka menenbi?

In cash | with credit card

накталай | карточка менен
naktalaj | kartotʃka menen

Do you want the receipt?

Сизге чек керекпи?
sizge tʃek kerekpi?

Yes, please.

Ооба, берип коюңузчу.
ooba, berip kojʉŋuzʧu.

No, it's OK.

Жок, кереги жок. Рахмат.
ʤok, keregi ʤok. raχmat.

Thank you. Have a nice day!

Рахмат. Жакшы калгыла.
raχmat. ʤakʃı kalgıla.

In town

Excuse me, ...	**Кечиресиз, ...** ketʃiresiz, ...
I'm looking for ...	**Мен ... издеп жаттым эле.** men ... izdep dʒattım ele.
the subway	**метрону** metronu
my hotel	**токтогон мейманканамды** toktogon mejmankanamdı
the movie theater	**кинотеатрды** kinoteatrdı
a taxi stand	**такси токтоочу жайды** taksi toktootʃu dʒajdı

an ATM	**банкоматты** bankomattı
a foreign exchange office	**акча алмаштыруу жайын** aktʃa almaʃtıruu dʒajın
an internet café	**интернет-кафени** internet-kafeni
... street	**... деген көчөнү** ... degen køtʃøny
this place	**ушул орунду** uʃul orundu

Do you know where ... is?	**Сиз ... каякта экенин билесизби?** siz ... kajakta ekenin bilesizbi?
Which street is this?	**Бул көчөнүн аталышы кандай?** bul køtʃønyn atalıʃı kandaj?
Show me where we are right now.	**Биз азыр кайсы жерде турабыз, көрсөтүп бериңизчи.** biz azır kajsı dʒerde turabız, børsøtyp beriŋiztʃi.
Can I get there on foot?	**Мен ал жакка жөө жете аламбы?** men al dʒakka dʒøø dʒete alambı?
Do you have a map of the city?	**Сизде шаардын картасы барбы?** sizde ʃaardın kartası barbı?

How much is a ticket to get in?	**Кирүү билети канча турат?** kiryy bileti kantʃa turat?
Can I take pictures here?	**Бул жерде сүрөткө тартууга болобу?** bul dʒerde syrøtkø tartuuga bolobu?

Are you open?

Силер иштейсинерби?
siler iʃtejsinerbi?

When do you open?

Силер канчада ачыласынар?
siler kantʃada atʃılasınar?

When do you close?

Силер канчага чейин иштейсинер?
siler kantʃaga tʃejin iʃtejsiner?

Money

money	**акча** aktʃa
cash	**накталай акча** naktalaj aktʃa
paper money	**кагаз акча** kagaz aktʃa
loose change	**майда акча** majda aktʃa
check | change | tip	**эсеп | ашкан акча | чайга** esep | aʃkan aktʃa | tʃajga

credit card	**кредит карточкасы** kredit kartotʃkası
wallet	**капчык** kaptʃık
to buy	**сатып алуу** satıp aluu
to pay	**төлөө** tøløø
fine	**айып** ajıp
free	**бекер** beker

Where can I buy ...?	**... каяктан сатып алсам болот?** ... kajaktan satıp alsam bolot?
Is the bank open now?	**Банк азыр ачыкпы?** bank azır atʃıkpı?
When does it open?	**Ал канчада ачылат?** al kantʃada atʃılat?
When does it close?	**Ал канчага чейин иштейт?** al kantʃaga tʃejin iʃtejt?

How much?	**Канча турат?** kantʃa turat?
How much is this?	**Бул канча турат?** bul kantʃa turat?
That's too expensive.	**Бул аябай кымбат.** bul ajabaj kımbat.

Excuse me, where do I pay?	**Кечиресиз, касса кайсы жакта?** ketʃiresiz, kassa kajsı dʒakta?
Check, please.	**Эсептеп коюңузчу.** eseptep kojuŋuztʃu.

Can I pay by credit card?	**Карточка менен төлөсөм болобу?** kartotʃka menen tøløsøm bolobu?
Is there an ATM here?	**Бул жерде банкомат барбы?** bul dʒerde bankomat barbı?
I'm looking for an ATM.	**Мага банкомат керек эле.** maga bankomat kerek ele.

I'm looking for a foreign exchange office.	**Мен акча алмаштыруу жайын издеп жаттым эле.** men aktʃa almaʃtıruu dʒajın izdep dʒattım ele.
I'd like to change ...	**Мен ... алмаштырайын дегем.** men ... almaʃtırajın degem.
What is the exchange rate?	**Алмаштыруунун курсу кандай?** almaʃtıruunun kursu kandaj?
Do you need my passport?	**Сизге менин паспортум керекпи?** sizge menin pasportum kerekpi?

Time

What time is it?	**Саат канча болду?** saat kantʃa boldu?
When?	**Качан?** katʃan?
At what time?	**Саат канчада?** saat kantʃada?
now | later | after …	**азыр | ананыраак | кийинчерээк …** azır | ananıraak | kijintʃereek …

one o'clock	**күндүзү саат бирде** kyndyzy saat birde
one fifteen	**бирден он беш мүнөт өткөндө** birden on beʃ mynøt øtkøndø
one thirty	**бир жарымда** bir dʒarımda
one forty-five	**экиге он беш мүнөт калганда** ekige on beʃ mynøt kalganda

one | two | three	**бир | эки | үч** bir | eki | ytʃ
four | five | six	**төрт | беш | алты** tørt | beʃ | altı
seven | eight | nine	**жети | сегиз | тогуз** dʒeti | segiz | toguz
ten | eleven | twelve	**он | он бир | он эки** on | on bir | on eki

in …	**… кийин** … kijin
five minutes	**беш мүнөт** beʃ mynøt
ten minutes	**он мүнөт** on mynøt
fifteen minutes	**он беш мүнөт** on beʃ mynøt
twenty minutes	**жыйырма мүнөт** dʒijirma mynøt
half an hour	**жарым саат** dʒarım saat
an hour	**бир сааттан** bir saattan

in the morning	**эртең менен** erteŋ menen
early in the morning	**таң эрте** taŋ erte
this morning	**бүгүн эртең менен** bygyn erteŋ menen
tomorrow morning	**эртең эртең менен** erteŋ erteŋ menen

in the middle of the day	**түштө** tyʃtø
in the afternoon	**түштөн кийин** tyʃtøn kijin
in the evening	**кечинде** ketʃinde
tonight	**бүгүн кечинде** bygyn ketʃinde

at night	**түндө** tyndø
yesterday	**кечээ** ketʃee
today	**бүгүн** bygyn
tomorrow	**эртең** erteŋ
the day after tomorrow	**бүрсүгүнү** byrsygyny

What day is it today?	**Бүгүн кайсы күн?** bygyn kajsı kyn?
It's …	**Бүгүн …** bygyn …
Monday	**дүйшөмбү** dyjʃømby
Tuesday	**шейшемби** ʃejʃembi
Wednesday	**шаршемби** ʃarʃembi

Thursday	**бейшемби** bejʃembi
Friday	**жума** dʒuma
Saturday	**ишенби** iʃenbi
Sunday	**жекшемби** dʒekʃembi

Greetings. Introductions

Hello.	**Саламатсызбы.**
	salamatsızbı.
Pleased to meet you.	**Сиз менен таанышканыбызга кубанычтамын.**
	siz menen taanıʃkanıbızga kubanıʧtamın.
Me too.	**Мен дагы.**
	men dagı.
I'd like you to meet ...	**Таанышып алгыла. Бул ...**
	taanıʃıp algıla. bul ...
Nice to meet you.	**Таанышканыбызга кубанычтамын.**
	taanıʃkanıbızga kubanıʧtamın.
How are you?	**Кандайсыз? Иштериңиз кандай?**
	kandajsız? iʃteriŋiz kandaj?
My name is ...	**Менин атым ...**
	menin atım ...
His name is ...	**Анын аты ...**
	anın atı ...
Her name is ...	**Анын аты ...**
	anın atı ...
What's your name?	**Сиздин атыңыз ким?**
	sizdin atıŋız kim?
What's his name?	**Анын аты ким?**
	anın atı kim?
What's her name?	**Анын аты ким?**
	anın atı kim?
What's your last name?	**Сиздин фамилияңыз кандай?**
	sizdin familijaŋız kandaj?
You can call me ...	**Мени ... десениз болот.**
	meni ... deseniz bolot.
Where are you from?	**Каяктан болосуз?**
	kajaktan bolosuz?
I'm from ...	**Мен ...**
	men ...
What do you do for a living?	**Сиз ким болуп иштейсиз?**
	siz kim bolup iʃtejsiz?
Who is this?	**Бул ким?**
	bul kim?
Who is he?	**Ал ким?**
	al kim?

Who is she?	**Ал ким?** al kim?
Who are they?	**Алар кимдер?** alar kimder?

This is ...	**Бул ...** bul ...
my friend (masc.)	**менин досум** menin dosum
my friend (fem.)	**менин курбум** menin kurbum
my husband	**менин күйөөм** menin kyjøøm
my wife	**менин аялым** menin ajalım

my father	**менин атам** menin atam
my mother	**менин апам** menin apam
my brother	**менин байкем** menin bajkem
my sister	**менин эжем** menin eʒem
my son	**менин уулум** menin uulum
my daughter	**менин кызым** menin kızım

This is our son.	**Бул биздин уулубуз.** bul bizdin uulubuz.
This is our daughter.	**Бул биздин кызыбыз.** bul bizdin kızıbız.
These are my children.	**Бул менин балдарым.** bul menin baldarım.
These are our children.	**Бул биздин балдарыбыз.** bul bizdin baldarıbız.

Farewells

Good bye!

Bye! (inform.)

Көрүшкөнчө!
køryʃkøntʃø!

Жакшы бар!
dʒakʃı bar!

See you tomorrow.

See you soon.

See you at seven.

Эртеңкиге чейин.
erteŋkige tʃejin.

Көрүшкөнгө чейин.
køryʃkøngø tʃejin.

Жетилерде жолугалы.
dʒetilerde dʒolugalı.

Have fun!

Talk to you later.

Have a nice weekend.

Good night.

Жакшы көңүл ачкыла!
dʒakʃı køŋyl atʃkıla!

Ананыраак сүйлөшөлү.
ananıraak syjløʃøly.

Эс алуу күндөр жакшы өтсүн.
es aluu kyndør dʒakʃı øtsyn.

Түнүң бейпил болсун.
tynyŋ bejpil bolsun.

It's time for me to go.

I have to go.

I will be right back.

Мен кетишим керек.
men ketiʃim kerek.

Мен кетишим керек.
men ketiʃim kerek.

Мен азыр келем.
men azır kelem.

It's late.

Кеч болуп кетти.
ketʃ bolup ketti.

I have to get up early.

Мен эртең эрте турушум керек.
men erteŋ erte turuʃum kerek.

I'm leaving tomorrow.

Мен эртең кеткени жатам.
men erteŋ ketkeni dʒatam.

We're leaving tomorrow.

Биз эртең кеткени жатабыз.
biz erteŋ ketkeni dʒatabız.

Have a nice trip!

Жолуңар шыдыр болсун!
dʒoluŋar ʃıdır bolsun!

It was nice meeting you.

Сиз менен таанышканыма кубанычтамын.
siz menen taanıʃkanıma kubanıtʃtamın.

It was nice talking to you.

Сиз менен баарлашканыма кубанычтамын.
siz menen baarlaʃkanıma kubanıtʃtamın.

Thanks for everything.

Баардыгына рахмат.
baardıgına raχmat.

I had a very good time.

Мен убакытты сонун өткөрдүм.
men ubakıttı sonun ötkørdym.

We had a very good time.

Биз убакытты сонун өткөрдүк.
biz ubakıttı sonun ötkørdyk.

It was really great.

Баары ойдогудай болду.
baarı ojdogudaj boldu.

I'm going to miss you.

Мен сагынам.
men sagınam.

We're going to miss you.

Биз сагынабыз.
biz sagınabız.

Good luck!

Ийгилик!
ijgilik!

Say hi to …

… салам айтып коюңуз.
… salam ajtıp kojuŋuz.

Foreign language

I don't understand.	**Мен түшүнбөй жатам.** men tyʃynbøj dʒatam.
Write it down, please.	**Жазып бериңизчи.** dʒazıp beriŋiztʃi.
Do you speak …?	**Сиз … сүйлөгөндү билесизби?** siz … syjløgøndy bilesizbi?

I speak a little bit of …	**Мен бир аз … билем.** men bir az … bilem.
English	**англисче** anglistʃe
Turkish	**түркчө** tyrktʃø
Arabic	**арабча** arabtʃa
French	**французча** frantsuztʃa

German	**немисче** nemistʃe
Italian	**италиялыкча** italijalıktʃa
Spanish	**испанча** ispantʃa
Portuguese	**португалча** portugaltʃa
Chinese	**кытайча** kıtajtʃa
Japanese	**япончо** japontʃo

Can you repeat that, please.	**Кайра кайталап коюңузчу.** kajra kajtalap kojuŋuztʃu.
I understand.	**Мен түшүнүп жатам.** men tyʃynyp dʒatam.
I don't understand.	**Мен түшүнбөй жатам.** men tyʃynbøj dʒatam.
Please speak more slowly.	**Жайыраак сүйлөңүзчү.** dʒajıraak syjløŋyztʃy.

Is that correct? (Am I saying it right?)	**Мындай туурабы?** mındaj tuurabı?
What is this? (What does this mean?)	**Бул эмне?** bul emne?

Apologies

Excuse me, please.	**Кечиресиз.** ketʃiresiz.
I'm sorry.	**Мен өкүнүп жатам.** men økynyp dʒatam.
I'm really sorry.	**Кечиресиз.** ketʃiresiz.
Sorry, it's my fault.	**Күнөөмдү мойнума алам.** **Күнөө менден кетти.** kynøømdy mojnuma alam. kynøø menden ketti.
My mistake.	**Менин жаңылыштыгым.** menin dʒaŋılıʃtıgım.
May I ...?	**Мен ... ?** men ... ?
Do you mind if I ...?	**Сиз каршы болбойсузбу, эгер мен ...?** siz karʃı bolbojsuzbu, eger men ...?
It's OK.	**Эчтеке болбойт.** etʃteke bolbojt.
It's all right.	**Баары жайында.** baarı dʒajında.
Don't worry about it.	**Эч капачылык жок.** etʃ kapatʃılık dʒok.

Agreement

Yes.	**Ооба.** ooba.
Yes, sure.	**Ооба, албетте.** ooba, albette.
OK (Good!)	**Макул!** makul!
Very well.	**Абдан жакшы.** abdan dʒakʃı.
Certainly!	**Албетте!** albette!
I agree.	**Мен макулмун.** men makulmun.

That's correct.	**Чын.** tʃın.
That's right.	**Туура.** tuura.
You're right.	**Сиз туура айтасыз.** siz tuura ajtasız.
I don't mind.	**Мен каршы эмесмин.** men karʃı emesmin.
Absolutely right.	**Туптуура.** tuptuura.

It's possible.	**Балким.** balkim.
That's a good idea.	**Бул жакшы.** bul dʒakʃı.
I can't say no.	**Жок дей албайм.** dʒok dey albajm.
I'd be happy to.	**Кубанычтамын.** kubanıtʃtamın.
With pleasure.	**Чын көңүлүм менен.** tʃın køŋylym menen.

Refusal. Expressing doubt

No.	**Жок.**
	ʤok.
Certainly not.	**Албетте жок.**
	albette ʤok.
I don't agree.	**Мен макул эмесмин.**
	men makul emesmin.
I don't think so.	**Мен антип ойлобойм.**
	men antip ojlobojm.
It's not true.	**Ишенбейм.**
	iʃenbejm.

You are wrong.	**Сиз туура эмес сүйлөп жатасыз.**
	siz tuura emes syjløp ʤatasız.
I think you are wrong.	**Менин оюмча, сиз жаңылышып жатасыз.**
	menin oʤumtʃa, siz ʤaŋılıʃıp ʤatasız.
I'm not sure.	**Билбейм, так айталбайм.**
	bilbejm, tak ajtalbajm.
It's impossible.	**Мындай мүмкүн эмес.**
	mındaj mymkyn emes.
Nothing of the kind (sort)!	**Болбогон кеп!**
	bolbogon kep!

The exact opposite.	**Тескерисинче!**
	teskerisintʃe!
I'm against it.	**Мен каршымын.**
	men karʃimin.
I don't care.	**Мага баары бир.**
	maga baarı bir.
I have no idea.	**Билбейм.**
	bilbejm.
I doubt it.	**Ушундай экенине күмөнүм бар.**
	uʃundaj ekenine kymønym bar.

Sorry, I can't.	**Кечиресиз, бирок мен анте албайм.**
	ketʃiresiz, birok men ante albajm.
Sorry, I don't want to.	**Кечиресиз, мен каалаган жокмун.**
	ketʃiresiz, men kaalagan ʤokmun.
Thank you, but I don't need this.	**Рахмат, мунун мага кереги жок.**
	raχmat, munun maga keregi ʤok.
It's getting late.	**Кеч болуп кетти.**
	ketʃ bolup ketti.

I have to get up early.

Мен эртең эрте турушум керек.
men erteŋ erte turuʃum kerek.

I don't feel well.

Мен өзүмдү жаман сезип жатам.
men øzymdy dʒaman sezip dʒatam.

Expressing gratitude

Thank you.	**Рахмат.** raχmat.
Thank you very much.	**Чоң рахмат.** ʧoŋ raχmat.
I really appreciate it.	**Чоң рахмат.** ʧoŋ raχmat.
I'm really grateful to you.	**Мен сизге ыраазымын.** men sizge ıraazımın.
We are really grateful to you.	**Биз сизге ыраазыбыз.** biz sizge ıraazıbız.

Thank you for your time.	**Убакыт бөлгөнүңүз үчүн рахмат.** ubakıt bølgønyŋyz ytʃyn raχmat.
Thanks for everything.	**Баардыгына рахмат.** baardıgına raχmat.
Thank you for ...	**... рахмат.** ... raχmat.
your help	**сиздин жардам бергениңиз үчүн** sizdin dʒardam bergeniŋiz ytʃyn
a nice time	**жакшы өткөргөн убакыт үчүн** dʒakʃı øtkørgøn ubakıt ytʃyn

a wonderful meal	**даамдуу тамак үчүн** daamduu tamak ytʃyn
a pleasant evening	**жагымдуу кече үчүн** dʒagımduu keʧe ytʃyn
a wonderful day	**сонун күн үчүн** sonun kyn ytʃyn
an amazing journey	**кызыктуу саякат үчүн** kızıktuu sajakat ytʃyn

Don't mention it.	**Эчтеке эмес.** etʃteke emes.
You are welcome.	**Рахмат айтуунун кажети жок.** raχmat ajtuunun kadʒeti dʒok.
Any time.	**Ар дайым даярмын.** ar dajım dajarmın.
My pleasure.	**Жардам бергенге кубанычтамын.** dʒardam bergenge kubanıʧtamın.
Forget it.	**Жөн коюңуз. Баары жайында** dʒøn kodʒıŋuz. baarı dʒajında
Don't worry about it.	**Эч капачылык жок.** etʃ kapaʧılık dʒok.

Congratulations. Best wishes

Congratulations!	**Куттуктайм!** kuttuktajm!
Happy birthday!	**Туулган күнүң менен!** tuulgan kynyŋ menen!
Merry Christmas!	**Рождество көңүлдүү өтсүн!** rodʒdestvo køŋyldyy øtsyn!
Happy New Year!	**Жаңы жылыңыздар менен!** dʒaŋı dʒılıŋızdar menen!
Happy Easter!	**Пасха майрамыңар менен!** pasχa majramıŋar menen!
Happy Hanukkah!	**Ханука майрамыңыздар кут болсун!** χanuka majramıŋızdar kut bolsun!
Cheers!	**Сиздин ден-соолугуңуз үчүн!** sizdin den-sooluguŋuz ytʃyn!
Let's drink to …!	**… үчүн алып жиберели!** … ytʃyn alıp dʒibereli!
To our success!	**Биздин ийгилигибиз үчүн!** bizdin ijgiligibiz ytʃyn!
To your success!	**Сиздин ийгилигиңиз үчүн!** sizdin ijgiliginiz ytʃyn!
Good luck!	**Ийгилик!** ijgilik!
Have a nice day!	**Күнүңүз куунак өтсүн!** kynyŋyz kuunak øtsyn!
Have a good holiday!	**Дем алуу күндөрүңүз жакшы өтсүн!** dem aluu kyndøryŋyz dʒakʃı øtsyn!
Have a safe journey!	**Жолуңуз шыдыр болсун!** dʒoluŋuz ʃıdır bolsun!
I hope you get better soon!	**Эртерээк сакайып кетишиңизди каалайм.** ertereek sakayıp ketiʃiŋizdi kaalajm.

Socializing

Why are you sad?	**Эмнеге көнүлүнүз жок?** emnege kөŋylyŋyz dʒok?
Smile! Cheer up!	**Күлүп коюнузчу!** kylyp kojuŋuztʃu!
Are you free tonight?	**Сиз бүгүн кечинде бошсузбу?** siz bygyn ketʃinde boʃsuzbu?

May I offer you a drink?	**Мен сизге ичимдик сунуш кылсам болобу?** men sizge itʃimdik sunuʃ kılsam bolobu?
Would you like to dance?	**Бийлегиниз келген жокпу?** bijleginiz kelgen dʒokpu?
Let's go to the movies.	**Балким киного барып келбейлиби?** balkim kinogo barıp kelbejlibi?

May I invite you to …?	**Мен сизди … чакырсам болобу?** men sizdi … tʃakırsam bolobu?
a restaurant	**ресторанга** restoranga
the movies	**киного** kinogo
the theater	**театрга** teatrga
go for a walk	**сейилдөөгө** sejildøøgø

At what time?	**Саат канчада?** saat kantʃada?
tonight	**бүгүн кечинде** bygyn ketʃinde
at six	**саат алтыда** saat altıda
at seven	**саат жетиде** saat dʒetide
at eight	**саат сегизде** saat segizde
at nine	**саат тогузда** saat toguzda

Do you like it here?	**Сизге бул жер жактыбы?** sizge bul dʒer dʒaktıbı?
Are you here with someone?	**Сиз бул жерде бирөө мененсизби?** siz bul dʒerde birøø menensizbi?

I'm with my friend.

Мен досум /кызым/ мененмин.
men dosum /kızım/ menenmin.

I'm with my friends.

Мен досторум мененмин.
men dostorum menenmin.

No, I'm alone.

Мен жалгызмын.
men dʒalgızmın.

Do you have a boyfriend?

Сенин сүйлөшкөн жигитиң барбы?
senin syjløʃkøn dʒigitiŋ barbı?

I have a boyfriend.

Менин досум бар.
menin dosum bar.

Do you have a girlfriend?

Сенин курбуң барбы?
senin kurbuŋ barbı?

I have a girlfriend.

Менин сүйлөшкөн кызым бар.
menin syjløʃkøn kızım bar.

Can I see you again?

Биз дагы жолугабызбы?
biz dagı dʒolugabızbı?

Can I call you?

Мен сага чалсам болобу?
men saga tʃalsam bolobu?

Call me. (Give me a call.)

Мага чалчы.
maga tʃaltʃı.

What's your number?

Сенин телефон номериң кандай?
senin telefon nomeriŋ kandaj?

I miss you.

Мен сени сагынып жатам.
men seni sagınıp dʒatam.

You have a beautiful name.

Атыңыз кандай сонун.
atıŋız kandaj sonun.

I love you.

Мен сени сүйөм.
men seni syjøm.

Will you marry me?

Мага турмушка чыгасыңбы?
maga turmuʃka tʃıgasıŋbı?

You're kidding!

Коюңузчу!
kojuŋuztʃu?

I'm just kidding.

Мен жөн эле тамашалап жатам.
men dʒøn ele tamaʃalap dʒatam.

Are you serious?

Сиз чын эле айтып жатасызбы?
siz tʃın ele ajtıp dʒatasızbı?

I'm serious.

Мен чын айтып жатам.
men tʃın ajtıp dʒatam.

Really?!

Чын элеби?!
tʃın elebi?!

It's unbelievable!

Мындай мүмкүн эмес.
mındaj mymkyn emes.

I don't believe you.

Мен сизге ишенбейм.
men sizge iʃenbejm.

I can't.

Мен анте албайм.
men ante albajm.

I don't know.

Мен билбейм.
men bilbejm.

I don't understand you.	**Сизди түшүнбөй турам.** sizdi tyʃynbøj turam.
Please go away.	**Кетиңизчи, суранам.** ketiŋizʧi, suranam.
Leave me alone!	**Мени өз жайыма койгулачы.** meni øz dʒajıma kojgulaʧı.

I can't stand him.	**Мен аны көргүм келбейт.** men anı kørgym kelbejt.
You are disgusting!	**Сизди көрөйүн деген көзүм жок!** sizdi kørøjyn degen køzym dʒok!
I'll call the police!	**Мен милицияны чакырам!** men militsijanı ʧakıram!

Sharing impressions. Emotions

I like it.	**Мага бул жакты.** maga bul dʒaktı.
Very nice.	**Жакшынакай экен.** dʒakʃınakaj eken.
That's great!	**Сонун экен!** sonun eken!
It's not bad.	**Жаман эмес.** dʒaman emes.

I don't like it.	**Мага бул жаккан жок.** maga bul dʒakkan dʒok.
It's not good.	**Бул жакшы эмес.** bul dʒakʃı emes.
It's bad.	**Бул жаман.** bul dʒaman.
It's very bad.	**Бул аябай жаман.** bul ajabaj dʒaman.
It's disgusting.	**Көңүлдү иренжиткен нерсе экен.** køŋyldy irendʒitken nerse eken.

I'm happy.	**Бактылуумун.** baktıluumun.
I'm content.	**Ыраазымын.** iraazımın.
I'm in love.	**Сүйүп калдым.** syjyp kaldım.
I'm calm.	**Тынч элемин.** tıntʃ elemin.
I'm bored.	**Зеригип жатам.** zerigip dʒatam.

I'm tired.	**Мен чарчадым.** men tʃartʃadım.
I'm sad.	**Көңүлүм болбой жатат.** køŋylym bolboj dʒatat.

I'm frightened.	**Жүрөгүм түшүп жатат.** dʒyrøgym tyʃyp dʒatat.
I'm angry.	**Жиним келип жатат.** dʒinim kelip dʒatat.
I'm worried.	**Тынчым кетип жатат.** tıntʃım ketip dʒatat.
I'm nervous.	**Нервим кайнап турат.** nervim kajnap turat.

I'm jealous. (envious)	**Ичим күйүп жатат.** itʃim kyjyp dʒatat.
I'm surprised.	**Таң калыштуу.** taŋ kalıʃtuu.
I'm perplexed.	**Мен эмне дээримди билбей жатам.** men emne deerimdi bilbej dʒatam.

Problems. Accidents

I've got a problem.

Менде көйгөй чыкты.
mende køygøj ʧıktı.

We've got a problem.

Бизде көйгөй чыкты.
bizde køjgøj ʧıktı.

I'm lost.

Мен адашып кеттим.
men adaʃıp kettim.

I missed the last bus (train).

Мен акыркы автобуска жетишпей калдым.
men akırkı avtobuska dʒetiʃpej kaldım.

I don't have any money left.

Менин таптакыр акчам жок калды.
menin taptakır akʧam dʒok kaldı.

I've lost my ...

Мен ... жоготуп алдым.
men ... dʒogotup aldım.

Someone stole my ...

Мен ... уурдатып ийдим.
men ... uurdatıp ijdim.

passport

паспортумду
pasportumdu

wallet

капчыгымды
kapʧıgımdı

papers

документтеримди
dokumentterimdi

ticket

билетимди
biletimdi

---

money

акчамды
akʧamdı

handbag

сумкамды
sumkamdı

camera

фотоаппаратымды
fotoapparatımdı

laptop

ноутбугумду
noutbugumdu

tablet computer

планшетимди
planʃetimdi

mobile phone

телефонумду
telefonumdu

Help me!

Жардамга!
dʒardamga!

What's happened?

Эмне болду?
emne boldu?

fire	**өрт** ørt
shooting	**атышуу** atıʃuu
murder	**өлтүрүү** øltyryy
explosion	**жарылуу** dʒarıluu
fight	**мушташ** muʃtaʃ

Call the police!	**Милицияны чакырып коюңузчу!** militsijanı tʃakırıp kojuŋuztʃu!
Please hurry up!	**Тезирээк, сураныч!** tezireek, suranıtʃ!
I'm looking for the police station.	**Мен милиция бөлүмүн издеп жаттым эле.** men militsija bølymyn izdep dʒattım ele.
I need to make a call.	**Мен чалышым керек.** men tʃalıʃım kerek.
May I use your phone?	**Телефон чалып алсам болобу?** telefon tʃalıp alsam bolobu?

I've been …	**Мени …** meni …
mugged	**тоноп кетишти** tonop ketiʃti
robbed	**мен уурдатып ийдим.** men uurdatıp ijdim.
raped	**зордуктап кетишти** zorduktap ketiʃti
attacked (beaten up)	**сабап кетишти.** sabap ketiʃti.

Are you all right?	**Баары жайындабы?** baarı dʒajındabı?
Did you see who it was?	**Ким экенин сиз көрдүңүзбү?** kim ekenin siz kørdyŋyzby?
Would you be able to recognize the person?	**Сиз аны тааный аласызбы?** siz anı taanıj alasızbı?
Are you sure?	**Аны так айта аласызбы?** anı tak ajta alasızbı?

Please calm down.	**Суранам, тынчтансаңыз.** suranam, tıntʃtansaŋız.
Take it easy!	**Жайыраак!** dʒajıraak!
Don't worry!	**Кам санабаңыз.** kam sanabaŋız.
Everything will be fine.	**Баары жакшы болот.** baarı dʒakʃı bolot.

Everything's all right.

Баары жайында.
baarı ʤajında.

Come here, please.

Бери келсеңиз.
beri kelseŋiz.

I have some questions for you.

Мен сизге бир нече суроом бар.
men sizge bir neʧe suroom bar.

Wait a moment, please.

Күтүп турсаңыз.
kytyp tursaŋız.

Do you have any I.D.?

Сиздин документтериңиз барбы?
sizdin dokumentteriŋiz barbı?

Thanks. You can leave now.

Рахмат. Сиз бара берсеңиз болот.
raχmat. siz bara berseŋiz bolot.

Hands behind your head!

Колуңузду башыңызга алыңыз!
koluŋuzdu baʃıŋızga alıŋız!

You're under arrest!

Сиз камакка алындыңыз!
siz kamakka alındıŋız!

Health problems

Please help me.	**Мага жардам берип коюнузчу.** maga dʒardam berip kodʒuŋuztʃu.
I don't feel well.	**Мен өзүмдү жаман сезип жатам.** men ɵzymdy dʒaman sezip dʒatam.
My husband doesn't feel well.	**Менин күйөөм өзүн жаман сезип жатат.** menin kyjɵɵm ɵzyn dʒaman sezip dʒatat.
My son ...	**Менин балам ...** menin balam ...
My father ...	**Менин атам ...** menin atam ...
My wife doesn't feel well.	**Менин аялым өзүн жаман сезип жатат.** menin ajalım ɵzyn dʒaman sezip jatat.
My daughter ...	**Менин кызым ...** menin kızım ...
My mother ...	**Менин апам ...** menin apam ...
I've got a ...	**Менин ... ооруп жатат.** menin ... oorup dʒatat.
headache	**башым** baʃım
sore throat	**тамагым** tamagım
stomach ache	**ичим** itʃim
toothache	**тишим** tiʃim
I feel dizzy.	**Менин башым айланып жатат.** menin baʃım ajlanıp dʒatat.
He has a fever.	**Анын дене табы көтөрүлүп жатат.** anın dene tabı kɵtɵrylyp dʒatat.
She has a fever.	**Анын дене табы көтөрүлүп жатат.** anın dene tabı kɵtɵrylyp dʒatat.
I can't breathe.	**Мен дем алалбай жатам.** men dem alalbaj dʒatam.
I'm short of breath.	**Мага дем жетпей жатат.** maga dem dʒetpej dʒatat.

I am asthmatic.

Менин астмам бар.
menin astmam bar.

I am diabetic.

Менин диабетим бар.
menin diabetim bar.

I can't sleep.

Менин уйкум качып жатат.
menin ujkum katʃıp dʒatat.

food poisoning

тамак-ашка уулануу
tamak-aʃka uulanuu

It hurts here.

Мобу жерим ооруп жатат.
mobu dʒerim oorup dʒatat.

Help me!

Жардамга!
dʒardamga!

I am here!

Мен бул жердемин!
men bul dʒerdemin!

We are here!

Биз бул жердебиз!
biz bul dʒerdebiz!

Get me out of here!

Мени чыгаргылачы!
meni tʃıgargılatʃı!

I need a doctor.

Мага доктур керек эле.
maga doktur kerek ele.

I can't move.

Мен кыймылдай албай жатам.
men kıjmıldaj albaj dʒatam.

I can't move my legs.

Мен бутумду сезбей жатам.
men butumdu sezbej dʒatam.

I have a wound.

Мен жарадармын.
men dʒaradarmın.

Is it serious?

Абалым аябай эле начарбы?
abalım ajabaj ele natʃarbı?

My documents are in my pocket.

Менин документтерим чөнтөгүмдө.
menin dokumentterim tʃөntөgүmdө.

Calm down!

Тынчтансаңыз!
tıntʃtansaŋız!

May I use your phone?

Телефон чалып алсам болобу?
telefon tʃalıp alsam bolobu?

Call an ambulance!

Тез жардамды чакырып коюңузчу!
tez dʒardamdı tʃakırıp kodʒuŋuztʃu!

It's urgent!

Тезирээк!
tezireek!

It's an emergency!

Тезирээк керек!
tezireek kerek!

Please hurry up!

Тезирээк, сураныч!
tezireek, suranıtʃ!

Would you please call a doctor?

Доктурду чакырып коюңузчу.
dokturdu tʃakırıp kojuŋuztʃu.

Where is the hospital?

Айтып коюңузчу, оорукана каякта?
ajtıp kojuŋuztʃu, oorukana kajakta?

How are you feeling?

Сиз өзүңүздү кандай сезип жатасыз?
siz özyŋyzdy kandaj sezip dʒatasız?

Are you all right?

Баары жайындабы?
baarı dʒajındabı?

What's happened?

Эмне болду?
emne boldu?

I feel better now.

Мен өзүмдү жакшы сезип калдым.
men özymdy dʒakʃı sezip kaldım.

It's OK.

Баары жайында.
baarı dʒajında.

It's all right.

Баары жакшы.
baarı dʒakʃı.

At the pharmacy

pharmacy (drugstore)	**дарыкана** darıkana
24-hour pharmacy	**күнү-түнү иштеген дарыкана** kyny-tyny iʃtegen darıkana
Where is the closest pharmacy?	**Жакын жерде дарыкана барбы?** dʒakın dʒerde darıkana barbı?

Is it open now?	**Азыр ал жак ачыкпы?** azır al dʒak atʃıkpı?
At what time does it open?	**Саат канчада ал жак ачылат?** saat kantʃada al dʒak atʃılat?
At what time does it close?	**Ал жак саат канчага чейин иштейт?** al dʒak saat kantʃaga tʃejin iʃtejt?

Is it far?	**Бул жерден алыспы?** bul dʒerden alıspı?
Can I get there on foot?	**Мен ал жакка жөө жете аламбы?** men al dʒakka dʒøø dʒete alambı?
Can you show me on the map?	**Ал жакты картадан көрсөтүп бериңизчи.** al dʒaktı kartadan kørsøtyp beriŋiztʃi.

Please give me something for ...	**Мага ... дарысын берип коёсузбу** maga ... darısın berip kojosuzbu
a headache	**баш оорунун** baʃ oorunun
a cough	**жөтөлдүн** dʒøtøldyn
a cold	**суук тийгендин** suuk tijgendin
the flu	**сасык тумоонун** sasık tumoonun

a fever	**дененин табын түшүрүүчү** denenin tabın tyʃyryytʃy
a stomach ache	**ич оорунун** itʃ oorunun
nausea	**жүрөк айлануунун** dʒyrøk ajlanuunun
diarrhea	**ич өткөндүн** itʃ øtkøndyn
constipation	**ич катуунун** itʃ katuunun

pain in the back	**белим ооруп жатат** belim oorup dʒatat
chest pain	**төшүм ооруп жатат** tøʃym oorup dʒatat
side stitch	**каптал жагым ооруп жатат** kaptal dʒagım oorup dʒatat
abdominal pain	**ичим ооруп жатат** itʃim oorup dʒatat

pill	**дары** darı
ointment, cream	**май** maj
syrup	**сироп** sirop
spray	**чачыратма** tʃatʃıratma
drops	**тамчылатма** tamtʃılatma

You need to go to the hospital.	**Сизге ооруканага баруу керек.** sizge oorukanaga baruu kerek.
health insurance	**камсыздандыруу күбөлүгү** kamsızdandıruu kybølygy
prescription	**рецепт** retsept
insect repellant	**курт-кумурскалардан сактоо** **каражаты** kurt-kumurskalardan saktoo karadʒatı
Band Aid	**лейкопластырь** lejkoplastırʲ

The bare minimum

Excuse me, ...	**Кечиресиз, ...** ketʃiresiz, ...
Hello.	**Саламатсызбы.** salamatsızbı.
Thank you.	**Рахмат.** raχmat.
Good bye.	**Көрүшкөнчө.** køryʃkønʧø.
Yes.	**Ооба.** ooba.
No.	**Жок.** dʒok.
I don't know.	**Мен билбейм.** men bilbejm.
Where? | Where to? | When?	**Каякта? | Каякка? | Качан?** kajakta? | kajakka? | katʃan?

I need ...	**Мага ... керек эле.** maga ... kerek ele.
I want ...	**Мен ... гым келет.** men ... gım kelet.
Do you have ...?	**Силерде ... барбы?** silerde ... barbı?
Is there a ... here?	**Бул жерде ... барбы?** bul dʒerde ... barbı?
May I ...?	**Мага ... болобу?** maga ... bolobu?
..., please (polite request)	**Сураныч** suranıʧ

I'm looking for ...	**Мен ... издеп жаттым эле.** men ... izdep dʒattım ele.
the restroom	**даараткана** daaratkana
an ATM	**банкомат** bankomat
a pharmacy (drugstore)	**дарыкана** darıkana
a hospital	**оорукана** oorukana
the police station	**милиция бөлүмү** militsija bølymy
the subway	**метро** metro

a taxi	**такси** taksi
the train station	**вокзал** vokzal

My name is ...	**Менин атым ...** menin atım ...
What's your name?	**Сиздин атыңыз ким?** sizdin atıŋız kim?
Could you please help me?	**Мага жардам берип коюнузчу.** maga dʒardam berip kodʒʉŋuztʃu.
I've got a problem.	**Менде көйгөй чыкты.** mende køygøj tʃıktı.
I don't feel well.	**Мен өзүмдү жаман сезип жатам.** men øzymdy dʒaman sezip dʒatam.
Call an ambulance!	**Тез жардамды чакырып коюнузчу!** tez dʒardamdı tʃakırıp kodʒʉŋuztʃu!
May I make a call?	**Телефон чалып алсам болобу?** telefon tʃalıp alsam bolobu?

I'm sorry.	**Кечирип коюнуз** ketʃirip kojʉŋuz
You're welcome.	**Эчтеке эмес** etʃteke emes

I, me	**мен** men
you (inform.)	**сен** sen
he	**ал** al
she	**ал** al
they (masc.)	**алар** alar
they (fem.)	**алар** alar
we	**биз** biz
you (pl)	**сиз** siz
you (sg, form.)	**Сиз** siz

ENTRANCE	**КИРҮҮ** kiryy
EXIT	**ЧЫГУУ** tʃıguu
OUT OF ORDER	**ИШТЕБЕЙТ** iʃtebejt
CLOSED	**ЖАБЫК** dʒabık

OPEN

АЧЫК
atʃık

FOR WOMEN

АЙЫМДАР ҮЧҮН
ajımdar ytʃyn

FOR MEN

ЭРКЕКТЕР ҮЧҮН
erkekter ytʃyn

TOPICAL VOCABULARY

This section contains more than 3,000 of the most important words.
The dictionary will provide invaluable assistance while traveling abroad, because frequently individual words are enough for you to be understood.
The dictionary includes a convenient transcription of each foreign word

T&P Books Publishing

VOCABULARY
CONTENTS

T&P Books Publishing

BASIC CONCEPTS

T&P Books Publishing

1. Pronouns

| I, me | мен, мага | men, maga |
| you | сен | sen |

he, she, it	ал	al
we	биз	biz
you (to a group)	силер	siler
you (polite, sing.)	сиз	siz
you (polite, pl)	сиздер	sizder
they	алар	alar

2. Greetings. Salutations

Hello! (fam.)	Салам!	salam!
Hello! (form.)	Саламатсызбы!	salamatsızbı!
Good morning!	Кутман таңыңыз менен!	kutman taŋıŋız menen!
Good afternoon!	Кутман күнүңүз менен!	kutman kynyŋyz menen!
Good evening!	Кутман кечиңиз менен!	kutman ketʃiŋiz menen!

to say hello	учурашуу	utʃuraʃuu
Hi! (hello)	Кандай!	kandaj!
greeting (n)	салам	salam
to greet (vt)	саламдашуу	salamdaʃuu
How are you?	Иштериң кандай?	iʃteriŋ kandaj?
How are you? (form.)	Иштериңиз кандай?	iʃteriŋiz kandaj?
How are you? (fam.)	Иштер кандай?	iʃter kandaj?
What's new?	Эмне жаңылык?	emne dʒaŋılık?

Bye-Bye! Goodbye!	Көрүшкөнчө!	køryʃkøntʃø!
See you soon!	Эмки жолукканга чейин!	emki dʒolukkanga tʃejin!
Farewell! (to a friend)	Кош бол!	koʃ bol!
Farewell! (form.)	кырк бир	kırk bir
to say goodbye	коштошуу	koʃtoʃuu
So long!	Жакшы кал!	dʒakʃı kal!

Thank you!	Рахмат!	raχmat!
Thank you very much!	Чоң рахмат!	tʃoŋ raχmat!
You're welcome	Эч нерсе эмес	etʃ nerse emes
Don't mention it!	Алкышка арзыбайт	alkıʃka arzıbajt
It was nothing	Эчтеке эмес.	etʃteke emes
Excuse me! (fam.)	Кечир!	ketʃir!
Excuse me! (form.)	Кечирип коюңузчу!	ketʃirip kojuŋuztʃu!

to excuse (forgive)	кечирүү	ketʃiryy
to apologize (vi)	кечирим суроо	ketʃirim suroo
My apologies	Кечирим сурайм.	ketʃirim surajm
I'm sorry!	Кечиресиз!	ketʃiresiz!
to forgive (vt)	кечирүү	ketʃiryy
It's okay! (that's all right)	Эч капачылык жок.	etʃ kapatʃılık dʒok
please (adv)	суранам	suranam
Don't forget!	Унутуп калбаңыз!	unutup kalbaŋız!
Certainly!	Албетте!	albette!
Of course not!	Албетте жок!	albette dʒok!
Okay! (I agree)	Макул!	makul!
That's enough!	Жетишет!	dʒetiʃet!

3. Questions

Who?	Ким?	kim?
What?	Эмне?	emne?
Where? (at, in)	Каерде?	kaerde?
Where (to)?	Каяка?	kajaka?
From where?	Каяктан?	kajaktan?
When?	Качан?	katʃan?
Why? (What for?)	Эмне үчүн?	emne ytʃyn?
Why? (~ are you crying?)	Эмнеге?	emnege?
What for?	Кайсы керекке?	kajsı kerekke?
How? (in what way)	Кандай?	kandaj?
What? (What kind of ...?)	Кайсы?	kajsı?
Which?	Кайсынысы?	kajsınısı?
To whom?	Кимге?	kimge?
About whom?	Ким жөнүндө?	kim dʒөnyndө?
About what?	Эмне жөнүндө?	emne dʒөnyndө?
With whom?	Ким менен?	kim menen?
How many? How much?	Канча?	kantʃa?
Whose?	Кимдики?	kimdiki?
Whose? (fem.)	Кимдики?	kimdiki?
Whose? (pl)	Кимдердики?	kimderdiki?

4. Prepositions

with (accompanied by)	менен	menen
without	-сыз, -сиз	-sız, -siz
to (indicating direction)	... кездей	... kөzdөj
about (talking ~ ...)	... жөнүндө	... dʒөnyndө
before (in time)	... астында	... astında
in front of ...	... алдында	... aldında

under (beneath, below)	... астында	... astında
above (over)	... өйдө	... øjdø
on (atop)	... үстүндө	... ystyndø
from (off, out of)	-дан	-dan
of (made from)	-дан	-dan

| in (e.g., ~ ten minutes) | ... ичинде | ... itʃinde |
| over (across the top of) | ... үстүнөн | ... ystynøn |

5. Function words. Adverbs. Part 1

Where? (at, in)	Каерде?	kaerde?
here (adv)	бул жерде	bul dʒerde
there (adv)	тээтигил жакта	teetigil dʒakta

| somewhere (to be) | бир жерде | bir dʒerde |
| nowhere (not in any place) | эч жакта | etʃ dʒakta |

| by (near, beside) | ... жанында | ... dʒanında |
| by the window | терезенин жанында | terezenin dʒanında |

Where (to)?	Каяка?	kajaka?
here (e.g., come ~!)	бери	beri
there (e.g., to go ~)	нары	narı
from here (adv)	бул жерден	bul dʒerden
from there (adv)	тигил жерден	tigil dʒerden

| close (adv) | жакын | dʒakın |
| far (adv) | алыс | alıs |

near (e.g., ~ Paris)	... тегерегинде	... tegereginde
nearby (adv)	жакын арада	dʒakın arada
not far (adv)	алыс эмес	alıs emes

left (adj)	сол	sol
on the left	сол жакта	sol dʒakta
to the left	солго	solgo

right (adj)	оң	oŋ
on the right	оң жакта	oŋ dʒakta
to the right	оңго	oŋgo

in front (adv)	астыда	astıda
front (as adj)	алдыңкы	aldıŋkı
ahead (the kids ran ~)	алдыга	aldıga

behind (adv)	артында	artında
from behind	артынан	artınan
back (towards the rear)	артка	artka
middle	ортосу	ortosu

in the middle	ортосунда	ortosunda
at the side	капталында	kaptalında
everywhere (adv)	бүт жерде	byt dʒerde
around (in all directions)	айланасында	ajlanasında

from inside	ичинде	itʃinde
somewhere (to go)	бир жерде	bir dʒerde
straight (directly)	түз	tyz
back (e.g., come ~)	кайра	kajra

| from anywhere | бир жерден | bir dʒerden |
| from somewhere | бир жактан | bir dʒaktan |

firstly (adv)	биринчиден	birintʃiden
secondly (adv)	экинчиден	ekintʃiden
thirdly (adv)	үчүнчүдөн	ytʃyntʃydøn

suddenly (adv)	күтпөгөн жерден	kytpøgøn dʒerden
at first (in the beginning)	башында	baʃında
for the first time	биринчи жолу	birintʃi dʒolu
long before ...	... алдында	... aldında
anew (over again)	башынан	baʃınan
for good (adv)	түбөлүккө	tybølykkø

never (adv)	эч качан	etʃ katʃan
again (adv)	кайра	kajra
now (at present)	эми	emi
often (adv)	көпчүлүк учурда	køptʃylyk utʃurda
then (adv)	анда	anda
urgently (quickly)	тезинен	tezinen
usually (adv)	көбүнчө	købyntʃø

by the way, ...	баса, ...	basa, ...
possibly	мүмкүн	mymkyn
probably (adv)	балким	balkim
maybe (adv)	ыктымал	ıktımal
besides ...	андан тышкары, ...	andan tıʃkarı, ...
that's why ...	ошондуктан ...	oʃonduktan ...
in spite of ...	... карабастан	... karabastan
thanks to ...	... күчү менен	... kytʃy menen

what (pron.)	эмне	emne
that (conj.)	эмне	emne
something	бир нерсе	bir nerse
anything (something)	бир нерсе	bir nerse
nothing	эч нерсе	etʃ nerse

who (pron.)	ким	kim
someone	кимдир бирөө	kimdir birøø
somebody	бирөө жарым	birøø dʒarım
nobody	эч ким	etʃ kim
nowhere (a voyage to ~)	эч жака	etʃ dʒaka

nobody's	эч кимдики	etʃ kimdiki
somebody's	биреенүкү	birøønyky
so (I'm ~ glad)	эми	emi
also (as well)	ошондой эле	oʃondoj ele
too (as well)	дагы	dagı

6. Function words. Adverbs. Part 2

Why?	Эмнеге?	emnege?
for some reason	эмнегедир	emnegedir
because ...	... себептен	... sebepten
for some purpose	эмне үчүндүр	emne ytʃyndyr
and	жана	dʒana
or	же	dʒe
but	бирок	birok
for (e.g., ~ me)	үчүн	ytʃyn
too (~ many people)	өтө эле	øtø ele
only (exclusively)	азыр эле	azır ele
exactly (adv)	так	tak
about (more or less)	болжол менен	boldʒol menen
approximately (adv)	болжол менен	boldʒol menen
approximate (adj)	болжолдуу	boldʒolduu
almost (adv)	дээрлик	deerlik
the rest	калганы	kalganı
the other (second)	башка	baʃka
other (different)	башка бөлөк	baʃka bøløk
each (adj)	ар бири	ar biri
any (no matter which)	баардык	baardık
many, much (a lot of)	көп	køp
many people	көбү	køby
all (everyone)	баары	baarı
in return for ...	... алмашуу	... almaʃuu
in exchange (adv)	ордуна	orduna
by hand (made)	колго	kolgo
hardly (negative opinion)	ишенүүгө болбойт	iʃenyygø bolbojt
probably (adv)	балким	balkim
on purpose (intentionally)	атайын	atajın
by accident (adv)	кокустан	kokustan
very (adv)	аябай	ajabaj
for example (adv)	мисалы	misalı
between	ортосунда	ortosunda
among	арасында	arasında

so much (such a lot)	**ошончо**	oʃontʃo
especially (adv)	**өзгөчө**	øzgøtʃø

NUMBERS. MISCELLANEOUS

T&P Books Publishing

0 zero	нөл	nøl
1 one	бир	bir
2 two	эки	eki
3 three	үч	ytʃ
4 four	төрт	tørt

5 five	беш	beʃ
6 six	алты	altı
7 seven	жети	dʒeti
8 eight	сегиз	segiz
9 nine	тогуз	toguz

10 ten	он	on
11 eleven	он бир	on bir
12 twelve	он эки	on eki
13 thirteen	он үч	on ytʃ
14 fourteen	он төрт	on tørt

15 fifteen	он беш	on beʃ
16 sixteen	он алты	on altı
17 seventeen	он жети	on dʒeti
18 eighteen	он сегиз	on segiz
19 nineteen	он тогуз	on toguz

20 twenty	жыйырма	dʒıjırma
21 twenty-one	жыйырма бир	dʒıjırma bir
22 twenty-two	жыйырма эки	dʒıjırma eki
23 twenty-three	жыйырма үч	dʒıjırma ytʃ

30 thirty	отуз	otuz
31 thirty-one	отуз бир	otuz bir
32 thirty-two	отуз эки	otuz eki
33 thirty-three	отуз үч	otuz ytʃ

40 forty	кырк	kırk
42 forty-two	кырк эки	kırk eki
43 forty-three	кырк үч	kırk ytʃ

50 fifty	элүү	elyy
51 fifty-one	элүү бир	elyy bir
52 fifty-two	элүү эки	elyy eki
53 fifty-three	элүү үч	elyy ytʃ
60 sixty	алтымыш	altımıʃ
61 sixty-one	алтымыш бир	altımıʃ bir

| 62 sixty-two | алтымыш эки | altımıʃ eki |
| 63 sixty-three | алтымыш үч | altımıʃ ytʃ |

70 seventy	жетимиш	dʒetimiʃ
71 seventy-one	жетимиш бир	dʒetimiʃ bir
72 seventy-two	жетимиш эки	dʒetimiʃ eki
73 seventy-three	жетимиш үч	dʒetimiʃ ytʃ

80 eighty	сексен	seksen
81 eighty-one	сексен бир	seksen bir
82 eighty-two	сексен эки	seksen eki
83 eighty-three	сексен үч	seksen ytʃ

90 ninety	токсон	tokson
91 ninety-one	токсон бир	tokson bir
92 ninety-two	токсон эки	tokson eki
93 ninety-three	токсон үч	tokson ytʃ

8. Cardinal numbers. Part 2

100 one hundred	бир жүз	bir dʒyz
200 two hundred	эки жүз	eki dʒyz
300 three hundred	үч жүз	ytʃ dʒyz
400 four hundred	төрт жүз	tørt dʒyz
500 five hundred	беш жүз	beʃ dʒyz

600 six hundred	алты жүз	altı dʒyz
700 seven hundred	жети жүз	dʒeti dʒyz
800 eight hundred	сегиз жүз	segiz dʒyz
900 nine hundred	тогуз жүз	toguz dʒyz

1000 one thousand	бир миң	bir miŋ
2000 two thousand	эки миң	eki miŋ
3000 three thousand	үч миң	ytʃ miŋ
10000 ten thousand	он миң	on miŋ
one hundred thousand	жүз миң	dʒyz miŋ
million	миллион	million
billion	миллиард	milliard

9. Ordinal numbers

first (adj)	биринчи	birintʃi
second (adj)	экинчи	ekintʃi
third (adj)	үчүнчү	ytʃyntʃy
fourth (adj)	төртүнчү	tørtyntʃy
fifth (adj)	бешинчи	beʃintʃi
sixth (adj)	алтынчы	altıntʃı
seventh (adj)	жетинчи	dʒetintʃi

eighth (adj)	**сегизинчи**	segizintʃi
ninth (adj)	**тогузунчу**	toguzuntʃu
tenth (adj)	**онунчу**	onuntʃu

T&P BOOKS

COLOURS. UNITS OF MEASUREMENT

T&P Books Publishing

10. Colors

color	түс	tys
shade (tint)	кошумча түс	koʃumtʃa tys
hue	кубулуу	kubuluu
rainbow	күндүн кулагы	kyndyn kulagı
white (adj)	ак	ak
black (adj)	кара	kara
gray (adj)	боз	boz
green (adj)	жашыл	dʒaʃıl
yellow (adj)	сары	sarı
red (adj)	кызыл	kızıl
blue (adj)	көк	køk
light blue (adj)	көгүлтүр	køgyltyr
pink (adj)	мала	mala
orange (adj)	кызгылт сары	kızgılt sarı
violet (adj)	сыя көк	sıja køk
brown (adj)	күрөң	kyrøŋ
golden (adj)	алтын түстүү	altın tystyy
silvery (adj)	күмүш өңдүү	kymyʃ øŋdyy
beige (adj)	сары боз	sarı boz
cream (adj)	саргылт	sargılt
turquoise (adj)	бирюза	biruza
cherry red (adj)	кочкул кызыл	kotʃkul kızıl
lilac (adj)	кызгылт көгүш	kızgılt køgyʃ
crimson (adj)	ачык кызыл	atʃık kızıl
light (adj)	ачык	atʃık
dark (adj)	күңүрт	kyŋyrt
bright, vivid (adj)	ачык	atʃık
colored (pencils)	түстүү	tystyy
color (e.g., ~ film)	түстүү	tystyy
black-and-white (adj)	ак-кара	ak-kara
plain (one-colored)	бир өңчөй түстө	bir øŋtʃøj tystø
multicolored (adj)	ар түрдүү түстө	ar tyrdyy tystø

11. Units of measurement

weight	салмак	salmak
length	узундук	uzunduk

width	жазылык	dʒazılık
height	бийиктик	bijiktik
depth	терендик	terendik
volume	көлөм	køløm
area	аянт	ajant

gram	грамм	gramm
milligram	миллиграмм	milligramm
kilogram	килограмм	kilogramm
ton	тонна	tonna
pound	фунт	funt
ounce	унция	untsija

meter	метр	metr
millimeter	миллиметр	millimetr
centimeter	сантиметр	santimetr
kilometer	километр	kilometr
mile	миля	milʲa

inch	дюйм	dʉjm
foot	фут	fut
yard	ярд	jard

square meter	квадраттык метр	kvadrattık metr
hectare	гектар	gektar
liter	литр	litr
degree	градус	gradus
volt	вольт	volʲt
ampere	ампер	amper
horsepower	ат күчү	at kytʃy

quantity	саны	sanı
a little bit of …	… бир аз	… bir az
half	жарым	dʒarım
dozen	он эки даана	on eki daana
piece (item)	даана	daana

| size | чоңдук | tʃoŋduk |
| scale (map ~) | өлчөмчен | øltʃømtʃen |

minimal (adj)	минималдуу	minimalduu
the smallest (adj)	эң кичинекей	eŋ kitʃinekej
medium (adj)	орточо	ortotʃo
maximal (adj)	максималдуу	maksimalduu
the largest (adj)	эң чоң	eŋ tʃoŋ

12. Containers

| canning jar (glass ~) | банка | banka |
| can | банка | banka |

bucket	чака	t͡ʃaka
barrel	бочка	bot͡ʃka
wash basin (e.g., plastic ~)	дагара	dagara
tank (100L water ~)	бак	bak
hip flask	фляжка	flʲad͡ʒka
jerrycan	канистра	kanistra
tank (e.g., tank car)	цистерна	t͡sɪsterna
mug	кружка	krud͡ʒka
cup (of coffee, etc.)	чөйчөк	t͡ʃøjt͡ʃøk
saucer	табак	tabak
glass (tumbler)	ыстакан	ɪstakan
wine glass	бокал	bokal
stock pot (soup pot)	мискей	miskej
bottle (~ of wine)	бөтөлкө	bøtølkø
neck (of the bottle, etc.)	оозу	oozu
carafe (decanter)	графин	grafin
pitcher	кумура	kumura
vessel (container)	идиш	idiʃ
pot (crock, stoneware ~)	карапа	karapa
vase	ваза	vaza
flacon, bottle (perfume ~)	флакон	flakon
vial, small bottle	кичине бөтөлкө	kit͡ʃine bøtølkø
tube (of toothpaste)	тюбик	tʉbik
sack (bag)	кап	kap
bag (paper ~, plastic ~)	пакет	paket
pack (of cigarettes, etc.)	пачке	pat͡ʃke
box (e.g., shoebox)	куту	kutu
crate	үкөк	ykøk
basket	себет	sebet

MAIN VERBS

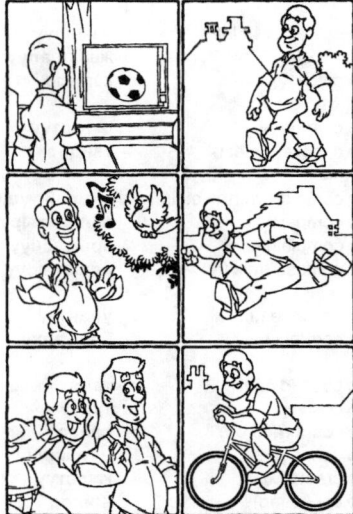

T&P Books Publishing

to advise (vt)	кеңеш берүү	keŋeʃ beryy
to agree (say yes)	макул болуу	makul boluu
to answer (vi, vt)	жооп берүү	dʒoop beryy
to apologize (vi)	кечирим суроо	ketʃirim suroo
to arrive (vi)	келүү	kelyy
to ask (~ oneself)	суроо	suroo
to ask (~ sb to do sth)	суроо	suroo
to be (vi)	болуу	boluu
to be afraid	жазкануу	dʒazkanuu
to be hungry	ачка болуу	atʃka boluu
to be interested in …	… кызыгуу	… kızıguu
to be needed	керек болуу	kerek boluu
to be surprised	таң калуу	taŋ kaluu
to be thirsty	суусап калуу	suusap kaluu
to begin (vt)	баштоо	baʃtoo
to belong to …	таандык болуу	taandık boluu
to boast (vi)	мактануу	maktanuu
to break (split into pieces)	сындыруу	sındıruu
to call (~ for help)	чакыруу	tʃakıruu
can (v aux)	жасай алуу	dʒasaj aluu
to catch (vt)	кармоо	karmoo
to change (vt)	өзгөртүү	øzgørtyy
to choose (select)	тандоо	tandoo
to come down (the stairs)	ылдый түшүү	ıldıj tyʃyy
to compare (vt)	салыштыруу	salıʃtıruu
to complain (vi, vt)	арыздануу	arızdanuu
to confuse (mix up)	адаштыруу	adaʃtıruu
to continue (vt)	улантуу	ulantuu
to control (vt)	башкаруу	baʃkaruu
to cook (dinner)	тамак бышыруу	tamak bıʃiruu
to cost (vt)	туруу	turuu
to count (add up)	саноо	sanoo
to count on …	… ишенүү	… iʃenyy
to create (vt)	жаратуу	dʒaratuu
to cry (weep)	ыйлоо	ıjloo

14. The most important verbs. Part 2

to deceive (vi, vt)	алдоо	aldoo
to decorate (tree, street)	кооздоо	koozdoo
to defend (a country, etc.)	коргоо	korgoo
to demand (request firmly)	талап кылуу	talap kıluu
to dig (vt)	казуу	kazuu
to discuss (vt)	талкуулоо	talkuuloo
to do (vt)	кылуу	kıluu
to doubt (have doubts)	күмөн саноо	kymøn sanoo
to drop (let fall)	түшүрүп алуу	tyʃyryp aluu
to enter (room, house, etc.)	кирүү	kiryy
to excuse (forgive)	кечирүү	ketʃiryy
to exist (vi)	чыгуу	tʃiguu
to expect (foresee)	күтүү	kytyy
to explain (vt)	түшүндүрүү	tyʃyndyryy
to fall (vi)	жыгылуу	dʒıgıluu
to find (vt)	таап алуу	taap aluu
to finish (vt)	бүтүрүү	bytyryy
to fly (vi)	учуу	utʃuu
to follow … (come after)	… ээрчүү	… eertʃyy
to forget (vi, vt)	унутуу	unutuu
to forgive (vt)	кечирүү	ketʃiryy
to give (vt)	берүү	beryy
to give a hint	четин чыгаруу	tʃetin tʃıgaruu
to go (on foot)	жөө басуу	dʒøø basuu
to go for a swim	сууга түшүү	suuga tyʃyy
to go out (for dinner, etc.)	чыгуу	tʃıguu
to guess (the answer)	жандырмагын табуу	dʒandırmagın tabuu
to have (vt)	бар болуу	bar boluu
to have breakfast	эртең менен тамактануу	erteŋ menen tamaktanuu
to have dinner	кечки тамакты ичүү	ketʃki tamaktı itʃyy
to have lunch	түштөнүү	tyʃtønyy
to hear (vt)	угуу	uguu
to help (vt)	жардам берүү	dʒardam beryy
to hide (vt)	жашыруу	dʒaʃıruu
to hope (vi, vt)	үмүттөнүү	ymyttønyy
to hunt (vi, vt)	аңчылык кылуу	aŋtʃılık kıluu
to hurry (vi)	шашуу	ʃaʃuu

15. The most important verbs. Part 3

to inform (vt)	маалымат берүү	maalımat beryy
to insist (vi, vt)	көшөрүү	køʃøryy
to insult (vt)	кемсинтүү	kemsintyy
to invite (vt)	чакыруу	tʃakıruu
to joke (vi)	тамашалоо	tamaʃaloo
to keep (vt)	сактоо	saktoo
to keep silent, to hush	үнчукпоо	untʃukpoo
to kill (vt)	өлтүрүү	øltyryy
to know (sb)	таануу	taanuu
to know (sth)	билүү	bilyy
to laugh (vi)	күлүү	kylyy
to liberate (city, etc.)	бошотуу	boʃotuu
to like (I like …)	жактыруу	dʒaktıruu
to look for … (search)	… издөө	… izdøø
to love (sb)	сүйүү	syjyy
to make a mistake	ката кетирүү	kata ketiryy
to manage, to run	башкаруу	baʃkaruu
to mean (signify)	билдирүү	bildiryy
to mention (talk about)	айтып өтүү	ajtıp øtyy
to miss (school, etc.)	калтыруу	kaltıruu
to notice (see)	байкоо	bajkoo
to object (vi, vt)	каршы болуу	karʃı bolu
to observe (see)	байкоо салуу	bajkoo
to open (vt)	ачуу	atʃuu
to order (meal, etc.)	буйрутма кылуу	bujrutma kıluu
to order (mil.)	буйрук кылуу	bujruk kıluu
to own (possess)	ээ болуу	ee boluu
to participate (vi)	катышуу	katıʃuu
to pay (vi, vt)	төлөө	tøløø
to permit (vt)	уруксат берүү	uruksat beryy
to plan (vt)	пландаштыруу	plandaʃtıruu
to play (children)	ойноо	ojnoo
to pray (vi, vt)	дуба кылуу	duba kıluu
to prefer (vt)	артык көрүү	artık køryy
to promise (vt)	убада берүү	ubada beryy
to pronounce (vt)	айтуу	ajtuu
to propose (vt)	сунуштоо	sunuʃtoo
to punish (vt)	жазалоо	dʒazaloo

16. The most important verbs. Part 4

to read (vi, vt)	окуу	okuu
to recommend (vt)	сунуштоо	sunuʃtoo

to refuse (vi, vt)	баш тартуу	baʃ tartuu
to regret (be sorry)	өкүнүү	økynyy
to rent (sth from sb)	батирге алуу	batirge aluu

to repeat (say again)	кайталоо	kajtaloo
to reserve, to book	камдык буйрутмалоо	kamdık bujrutmaloo
to run (vi)	чуркоо	tʃurkoo
to save (rescue)	куткаруу	kutkaruu
to say (~ thank you)	айтуу	ajtuu

to scold (vt)	урушуу	uruʃuu
to see (vt)	көрүү	køryy
to sell (vt)	сатуу	satuu
to send (vt)	жөнөтүү	dʒønøtyy
to shoot (vi)	атуу	atuu

to shout (vi)	кыйкыруу	kıjkıruu
to show (vt)	көрсөтүү	børsøtyy
to sign (document)	кол коюу	kol kojʉu
to sit down (vi)	отуруу	oturuu

to smile (vi)	жылмаюу	dʒılmadʒʉu
to speak (vi, vt)	сүйлөө	syjløø
to steal (money, etc.)	уурдоо	uurdoo
to stop (for pause, etc.)	токтоо	toktoo
to stop (please ~ calling me)	токтотуу	toktotuu

to study (vt)	окуу	okuu
to swim (vi)	сүзүү	syzyy
to take (vt)	алуу	aluu
to think (vi, vt)	ойлоо	ojloo
to threaten (vt)	коркутуу	korkutuu

to touch (with hands)	тийүү	tijyy
to translate (vt)	которуу	kotoruu
to trust (vt)	ишенүү	iʃenyy
to try (attempt)	аракет кылуу	araket kıluu
to turn (e.g., ~ left)	бурулуу	buruluu

to underestimate (vt)	баалабоо	baalaboo
to understand (vt)	түшүнүү	tyʃynyy
to unite (vt)	бириктирүү	biriktiryy
to wait (vt)	күтүү	kytyy

to want (wish, desire)	каалоо	kaaloo
to warn (vt)	эскертүү	eskertyy
to work (vi)	иштөө	iʃtøø
to write (vt)	жазуу	dʒazuu
to write down	кагазга түшүрүү	kagazga tyʃyryy

T&P BOOKS

TIME. CALENDAR

T&P Books Publishing

17. Weekdays

Monday	дүйшөмбү	dyjʃømby
Tuesday	шейшемби	ʃejʃembi
Wednesday	шаршемби	ʃarʃembi
Thursday	бейшемби	bejʃembi
Friday	жума	dʒuma
Saturday	ишенби	iʃenbi
Sunday	жекшемби	dʒekʃembi

today (adv)	бүгүн	bygyn
tomorrow (adv)	эртең	erteŋ
the day after tomorrow	бирсүгүнү	birsygyny
yesterday (adv)	кечээ	ketʃee
the day before yesterday	мурда күнү	murda kyny

day	күн	kyn
working day	иш күнү	iʃ kyny
public holiday	майрам күнү	majram kyny
day off	дем алыш күн	dem alıʃ kyn
weekend	дем алыш күндөр	dem alıʃ kyndør

all day long	күнү бою	kyny bojʉ
the next day (adv)	кийинки күнү	kijinki kyny
two days ago	эки күн мурун	eki kyn murun
the day before	жакында	dʒakında
daily (adj)	күндө	kyndø
every day (adv)	күн сайын	kyn sajın

week	жума	dʒuma
last week (adv)	өткөн жумада	øtkøn dʒumada
next week (adv)	келаткан жумада	kelatkan dʒumada
weekly (adj)	жума сайын	dʒuma sajın
every week (adv)	жума сайын	dʒuma sajın
twice a week	жумасына эки жолу	dʒumasına eki dʒolu
every Tuesday	ар шейшемби	ar ʃejʃembi

18. Hours. Day and night

morning	таң	taŋ
in the morning	эртең менен	erteŋ menen
noon, midday	жарым күн	dʒarım kyn
in the afternoon	түштөн кийин	tyʃtøn kijin
evening	кеч	ketʃ

98

in the evening	кечинде	ketʃinde
night	түн	tyn
at night	түндө	tyndø
midnight	жарым түн	dʒarım tyn

second	секунда	sekunda
minute	мүнөт	mynøt
hour	саат	saat
half an hour	жарым саат	dʒarım saat
a quarter-hour	чейрек саат	tʃejrek saat
fifteen minutes	он беш мүнөт	on beʃ mynøt
24 hours	сутка	sutka

sunrise	күндүн чыгышы	kyndyn tʃıgıʃı
dawn	таң агаруу	taŋ agaruu
early morning	таң эрте	taŋ erte
sunset	күн батуу	kyn batuu

early in the morning	таң эрте	taŋ erte
this morning	бүгүн эртең менен	bygyn erteŋ menen
tomorrow morning	эртең эртең менен	erteŋ erteŋ menen

this afternoon	күндүзү	kyndyzy
in the afternoon	түштөн кийин	tyʃtøn kijin
tomorrow afternoon	эртең түштөн кийин	erteŋ tyʃtøn kijin

| tonight (this evening) | бүгүн кечинде | bygyn ketʃinde |
| tomorrow night | эртең кечинде | erteŋ ketʃinde |

at 3 o'clock sharp	туура саат үчтө	tuura saat ytʃtø
about 4 o'clock	болжол менен төрт саат	boldʒol menen tørt saat
by 12 o'clock	саат он экиде	saat on ekide

in 20 minutes	жыйырма мүнөттөн кийин	dʒıjırma mynøttøn kijin
in an hour	бир сааттан кийин	bir saattan kijin
on time (adv)	өз убагында	øz ubagında

a quarter to …	… он беш мүнөт калды	… on beʃ mynøt kaldı
within an hour	бир сааттын ичинде	bir saattın itʃinde
every 15 minutes	он беш мүнөт сайын	on beʃ mynøt sajın
round the clock	бир сутка бою	bir sutka boju

19. Months. Seasons

January	январь	janvarʲ
February	февраль	fevralʲ
March	март	mart
April	апрель	aprelʲ

May	май	maj
June	июнь	ijunʲ
July	июль	ijulʲ
August	август	avgust
September	сентябрь	sentʲabrʲ
October	октябрь	oktʲabrʲ
November	ноябрь	nojabrʲ
December	декабрь	dekabrʲ
spring	жаз	dʒaz
in spring	жазында	dʒazında
spring (as adj)	жазгы	dʒazgı
summer	жай	dʒaj
in summer	жайында	dʒajında
summer (as adj)	жайкы	dʒajkı
fall	күз	kyz
in fall	күзүндө	kyzyndø
fall (as adj)	күздүк	kyzdyk
winter	кыш	kıʃ
in winter	кышында	kıʃında
winter (as adj)	кышкы	kıʃkı
month	ай	aj
this month	ушул айда	uʃul ajda
next month	кийинки айда	kijinki ajda
last month	өткөн айда	øtkøn ajda
a month ago	бир ай мурун	bir aj murun
in a month (a month later)	бир айдан кийин	bir ajdan kijin
in 2 months (2 months later)	эки айдан кийин	eki ajdan kijin
the whole month	ай бою	aj bojʉ
all month long	толук бир ай	toluk bir aj
monthly (~ magazine)	ай сайын	aj sajın
monthly (adv)	ай сайын	aj sajın
every month	ар бир айда	ar bir ajda
twice a month	айына эки жолу	ajına eki dʒolu
year	жыл	dʒıl
this year	бул жылы	bul dʒılı
next year	келаткан жылы	kelatkan dʒılı
last year	өткөн жылы	øtkøn dʒılı
a year ago	бир жыл мурун	bir dʒıl murun
in a year	бир жылдан кийин	bir dʒıldan kijin
in two years	эки жылдан кийин	eki dʒıldan kijin
the whole year	жыл бою	dʒıl bodʒʉ

all year long	толук бир жыл	toluk bir dʒıl
every year	ар жыл сайын	ar dʒıl sajın
annual (adj)	жыл сайын	dʒıl sajın
annually (adv)	жыл сайын	dʒıl sajın
4 times a year	жылына төрт жолу	dʒılına tørt dʒolu
date (e.g., today's ~)	число	tʃislo
date (e.g., ~ of birth)	күн	kyn
calendar	календарь	kalendarʲ
half a year	жарым жыл	dʒarım dʒıl
six months	жарым чейрек	dʒarım tʃejrek
season (summer, etc.)	мезгил	mezgil
century	кылым	kılım

T&P BOOKS

TRAVEL. HOTEL

T&P Books Publishing

tourism, travel	туризм	turizm
tourist	турист	turist
trip, voyage	саякат	sajakat
adventure	укмуштуу окуя	ukmuʃtuu okuja
trip, journey	сапар	sapar

vacation	дем алыш	dem alıʃ
to be on vacation	дем алышка чыгуу	dem alıʃka tʃıguu
rest	эс алуу	es aluu

train	поезд	poezd
by train	поезд менен	poezd menen
airplane	учак	utʃak
by airplane	учакта	utʃakta
by car	автомобилде	avtomobilde
by ship	кемеде	kemede

luggage	жүк	dʒүk
suitcase	чемодан	tʃemodan
luggage cart	араба	araba
passport	паспорт	pasport
visa	виза	viza
ticket	билет	bilet
air ticket	авиабилет	aviabilet

guidebook	жол көрсөткүч	dʒol kөrsөtkytʃ
map (tourist ~)	карта	karta
area (rural ~)	жай	dʒaj
place, site	жер	dʒer

exotica (n)	экзотика	ekzotika
exotic (adj)	экзотикалуу	ekzotikaluu
amazing (adj)	ажайып	adʒajıp

group	топ	top
excursion, sightseeing tour	экскурсия	ekskursija
guide (person)	экскурсия жетекчиси	ekskursija dʒetektʃisi

| hotel, inn | мейманкана | mejmankana |
| motel | мотель | motelʲ |

three-star (~ hotel)	үч жылдыздуу	ytʃ dʒɯldɯzduu
five-star	беш жылдыздуу	beʃ dʒɯldɯzduu
to stay (in a hotel, etc.)	токтоо	toktoo

room	номер	nomer
single room	бир орундуу	bir orunduu
double room	эки орундуу	eki orunduu
to book a room	номерди камдык буйрутмалоо	nomerdi kamdık bujrutmaloo

| half board | жарым пансион | dʒarım pansion |
| full board | толук пансион | toluk pansion |

with bath	ваннасы менен	vannası menen
with shower	душ менен	duʃ menen
satellite television	спутник	sputnik
air-conditioner	аба желдеткич	aba dʒeldetkitʃ
towel	сүлгү	sylgy
key	ачкыч	atʃkɯtʃ

administrator	администратор	administrator
chambermaid	үй кызматкери	yj kızmatkeri
porter, bellboy	жүк ташуучу	dʒyk taʃuutʃu
doorman	эшик ачуучу	eʃik atʃuutʃu

restaurant	ресторан	restoran
pub, bar	бар	bar
breakfast	таңкы тамак	taŋkı tamak
dinner	кечки тамак	ketʃki tamak
buffet	шведче стол	ʃvedtʃe stol

| lobby | вестибюль | vestibʉlʲ |
| elevator | лифт | lift |

| DO NOT DISTURB | ТЫНЧЫБЫЗДЫ АЛБАГЫЛА! | tıntʃıbızdı albagıla! |
| NO SMOKING | ТАМЕКИ ЧЕГҮҮГӨ БОЛБОЙТ! | tameki tʃegyygø bolbojt! |

22. Sightseeing

monument	эстелик	estelik
fortress	чеп	tʃep
palace	сарай	saraj
castle	сепил	sepil
tower	мунара	munara
mausoleum	күмбөз	kymbøz

| architecture | архитектура | arχitektura |
| medieval (adj) | орто кылымдык | orto kılımdık |

ancient (adj)	**байыркы**	bajırkı
national (adj)	**улуттук**	uluttuk
famous (monument, etc.)	**таанымал**	taanımal
tourist	**турист**	turist
guide (person)	**гид**	gid
excursion, sightseeing tour	**экскурсия**	ekskursija
to show (vt)	**көрсөтүү**	kørsøtyy
to tell (vt)	**айтып берүү**	ajtıp beryy
to find (vt)	**табуу**	tabuu
to get lost (lose one's way)	**адашып кетүү**	adaʃıp ketyy
map (e.g., subway ~)	**схема**	sχema
map (e.g., city ~)	**план**	plan
souvenir, gift	**асембелек**	asembelek
gift shop	**асембелек дүкөнү**	asembelek dykøny
to take pictures	**сүрөткө тартуу**	syrøtkø tartuu
to have one's picture taken	**сүрөткө түшүү**	syrøtkø tyʃyy

T&P BOOKS

TRANSPORTATION

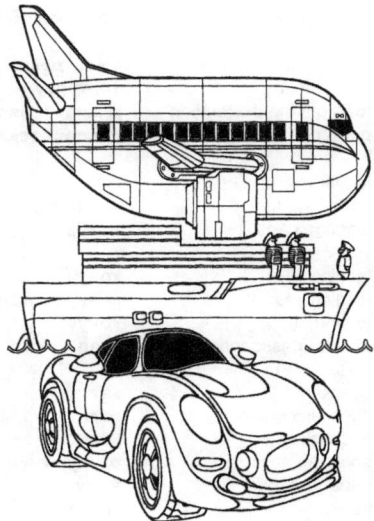

T&P Books Publishing

23. Airport

airport	аэропорт	aeroport
airplane	учак	utʃak
airline	авиакомпания	aviakompanija
air traffic controller	авиадиспетчер	aviadispettʃer

departure	учуп кетүү	utʃup ketyy
arrival	учуп келүү	utʃup kelyy
to arrive (by plane)	учуп келүү	utʃup kelyy

| departure time | учуп кетүү убактысы | utʃup ketyy ubaktısı |
| arrival time | учуп келүү убактысы | utʃup kelyy ubaktısı |

| to be delayed | кармалуу | karmaluu |
| flight delay | учуп кетүүнүн кечигиши | utʃup ketyynyn ketʃigiʃi |

information board	маалымат таблосу	maalımat tablosu
information	маалымат	maalımat
to announce (vt)	кулактандыруу	kulaktandıruu
flight (e.g., next ~)	рейс	rejs

| customs | бажыкана | badʒıkana |
| customs officer | бажы кызматкери | badʒı kızmatkeri |

customs declaration	бажы декларациясы	badʒı deklaratsijası
to fill out (vt)	толтуруу	tolturuu
to fill out the declaration	декларация толтуруу	deklaratsija tolturuu
passport control	паспорт текшерүү	pasport tekʃeryy

luggage	жүк	dʒyk
hand luggage	кол жүгү	kol dʒygy
luggage cart	араба	araba

landing	конуу	konuu
landing strip	конуу тилкеси	konuu tilkesi
to land (vi)	конуу	konuu
airstair (passenger stair)	трап	trap

check-in	катталуу	kattaluu
check-in counter	каттоо стойкасы	kattoo stojkası
to check-in (vi)	катталуу	kattaluu
boarding pass	отуруу үчүн талон	oturuu ytʃyn talon
departure gate	чыгуу	tʃıguu
transit	транзит	tranzit

to wait (vt)	күтүү	kytyy
departure lounge	күтүү залы	kutyy zalı
to see off	узатуу	uzatuu
to say goodbye	коштошуу	koʃtoʃuu

24. Airplane

airplane	учак	utʃak
air ticket	авиабилет	aviabilet
airline	авиакомпания	aviakompanija
airport	аэропорт	aeroport
supersonic (adj)	сверхзвуковой	sverχzvukovoj

captain	кеме командири	keme komandiri
crew	экипаж	ekipadʒ
pilot	учкуч	utʃkutʃ
flight attendant (fem.)	стюардесса	stuardessa
navigator	штурман	ʃturman

wings	канаттар	kanattar
tail	куйрук	kujruk
cockpit	кабина	kabina
engine	кыймылдаткыч	kıjmıldatkıtʃ
undercarriage (landing gear)	шасси	ʃassi
turbine	турбина	turbina

propeller	пропеллер	propeller
black box	кара куту	kara kutu
yoke (control column)	штурвал	ʃturval
fuel	күйүүчү май	kyjyytʃy may

safety card	коопсуздук көрсөтмөсү	koopsuzduk kørsøtmøsy
oxygen mask	кислород чүмбөтү	kislorod tʃymbøty
uniform	бир беткей кийим	bir betkey kijim
life vest	куткаруучу күрмө	kutkaruutʃu kyrmø
parachute	парашют	paraʃut

takeoff	учуп көтөрүлүү	utʃup køtørylyy
to take off (vi)	учуп көтөрүлүү	utʃup køtørylyy
runway	учуп чыгуу тилкеси	utʃup tʃıguu tilkesi

visibility	көрүнүш	kørynyʃ
flight (act of flying)	учуу	utʃuu
altitude	бийиктик	bijiktik
air pocket	аба чүңкуру	aba tʃyŋkuru

seat	орун	orun
headphones	кулакчын	kulaktʃın
folding tray (tray table)	бүктөлмө стол	byktølmø stol

| airplane window | иллюминатор | illuminator |
| aisle | өтмөк | øtmøk |

25. Train

train	поезд	poezd
commuter train	электричка	elektritʃka
express train	бат жүрүүчү поезд	bat dʒyryytʃy poezd
diesel locomotive	тепловоз	teplovoz
steam locomotive	паровоз	parovoz

| passenger car | вагон | vagon |
| dining car | вагон-ресторан | vagon-restoran |

rails	рельсалар	relʲsalar
railroad	темир жолу	temir dʒolu
railway tie	шпала	ʃpala

platform (railway ~)	платформа	platforma
track (~ 1, 2, etc.)	жол	dʒol
semaphore	семафор	semafor
station	бекет	beket

engineer (train driver)	машинист	maʃinist
porter (of luggage)	жук ташуучу	dʒuk taʃuutʃu
car attendant	проводник	provodnik
passenger	жүргүнчү	dʒyrgyntʃy
conductor (ticket inspector)	текшерүүчү	tekʃeryytʃy

| corridor (in train) | коридор | koridor |
| emergency brake | стоп-кран | stop-kran |

compartment	купе	kupe
berth	текче	tektʃe
upper berth	үстүңкү текче	ystyŋky tektʃe
lower berth	ылдыйкы текче	ıldıjkı tektʃe
bed linen, bedding	жууркан-төшөк	dʒuurkan-tøʃøk

ticket	билет	bilet
schedule	ыраттама	ıraattama
information display	табло	tablo

to leave, to depart	жөнөө	dʒønøø
departure (of train)	жөнөө	dʒønøø
to arrive (ab. train)	келүү	kelyy
arrival	келүү	kelyy

| to arrive by train | поезд менен келүү | poezd menen kelyy |
| to get on the train | поездге отуруу | poezdge oturuu |

to get off the train	поездден түшүү	poezdden tyſyy
train wreck	кыйроо	kıjroo
to derail (vi)	рельсадан чыгып кетүү	relʲsadan ʧıgıp ketyy

steam locomotive	паровоз	parovoz
stoker, fireman	от жагуучу	ot ʤaguutʃu
firebox	меш	meʃ
coal	көмүр	kømyr

26. Ship

| ship | кеме | keme |
| vessel | кеме | keme |

steamship	пароход	paroχod
riverboat	теплоход	teploχod
cruise ship	лайнер	lajner
cruiser	крейсер	krejser

yacht	яхта	jaχta
tugboat	буксир	buksir
barge	баржа	barʤa
ferry	паром	parom

| sailing ship | парус | parus |
| brigantine | бригантина | brigantina |

| ice breaker | муз жаргыч кеме | muz ʤargıʧ keme |
| submarine | суу астында жүрүүчү кеме | suu astında ʤyryytʃy keme |

boat (flat-bottomed ~)	кайык	kajık
dinghy	шлюпка	ʃlʉpka
lifeboat	куткаруу шлюпкасы	kutkaruu ʃlʉpkası
motorboat	катер	kater

captain	капитан	kapitan
seaman	матрос	matros
sailor	деңизчи	deŋiztʃi
crew	экипаж	ekipaʤ

boatswain	боцман	boʦman
ship's boy	юнга	jʉnga
cook	кок	kok
ship's doctor	кеме доктуру	keme dokturu

deck	палуба	paluba
mast	мачта	matʃta
sail	парус	parus
hold	трюм	trʉm

bow (prow)	тумшук	tumʃuk
stern	кеменин арткы бөлүгү	kemenin artkı bølygy
oar	калак	kalak
screw propeller	винт	vint
cabin	каюта	kajʉta
wardroom	кают-компания	kajʉt-kompanija
engine room	машина бөлүгү	maʃina bølygy
bridge	капитан мостиги	kapitan mostigi
radio room	радиорубка	radiorubka
wave (radio)	толкун	tolkun
logbook	кеме журналы	keme dʒurnalı
spyglass	дүрбү	dyrby
bell	коңгуроо	konguroo
flag	байрак	bajrak
hawser (mooring ~)	аркан	arkan
knot (bowline, etc.)	түйүн	tyjyn
deckrails	туткуч	tutkutʃ
gangway	трап	trap
anchor	кеме казык	keme kazık
to weigh anchor	кеме казыкты көтөрүү	keme kazıktı køtøryy
to drop anchor	кеме казыкты таштоо	keme kazıktı taʃtoo
anchor chain	казык чынжыры	kazık tʃındʒırı
port (harbor)	порт	port
quay, wharf	причал	pritʃal
to berth (moor)	келип токтоо	kelip toktoo
to cast off	жээктен алыстоо	dʒeekten alıstoo
trip, voyage	саякат	sajakat
cruise (sea trip)	деңиз саякаты	deŋiz sajakatı
course (route)	курс	kurs
route (itinerary)	каттам	kattam
fairway (safe water channel)	фарватер	farvater
shallows	тайыз жер	tajız dʒer
to run aground	тайыз жерге отуруу	tajız dʒerge oturuu
storm	бороон чапкын	boroon tʃapkın
signal	сигнал	signal
to sink (vi)	чөгүү	tʃøgyy
Man overboard!	Сууда адам бар!	suuda adam bar!
SOS (distress signal)	SOS	sos
ring buoy	куткаруучу тегерек	kutkaruutʃu tegerek

T&P BOOKS

CITY

T&P Books Publishing

bus	автобус	avtobus
streetcar	трамвай	tramvaj
trolley bus	троллейбус	trollejbus
route (of bus, etc.)	каттам	kattam
number (e.g., bus ~)	номер	nomer
to go by ...	... жүрүү	... dʒyryy
to get on (~ the bus)	... отуруу	... oturuu
to get off ...	... түшүп калуу	... tyʃyp kaluu
stop (e.g., bus ~)	аялдама	ajaldama
next stop	кийинки аялдама	kijinki ajaldama
terminus	акыркы аялдама	akɪrkɪ ajaldama
schedule	ырааттама	ɪraattama
to wait (vt)	күтүү	kytyy
ticket	билет	bilet
fare	билеттин баасы	bilettin baasɪ
cashier (ticket seller)	кассир	kassir
ticket inspection	текшерүү	tekʃeryy
ticket inspector	текшерүүчү	tekʃeryytʃy
to be late (for ...)	кечигүү	ketʃigyy
to miss (~ the train, etc.)	кечигип калуу	ketʃigip kaluu
to be in a hurry	шашуу	ʃaʃuu
taxi, cab	такси	taksi
taxi driver	такси айдоочу	taksi ajdootʃu
by taxi	таксиде	takside
taxi stand	такси токтоочу жай	taksi toktootʃu dʒaj
to call a taxi	такси чакыруу	taksi tʃakɪruu
to take a taxi	такси кармоо	taksi karmoo
traffic	көчө кыймылы	køtʃø kɪjmɪlɪ
traffic jam	тыгын	tɪgɪn
rush hour	кызуу маал	kɪzuu maal
to park (vi)	токтотуу	toktotuu
to park (vt)	машинаны жайлаштыруу	maʃinanɪ dʒajlaʃtɪruu
parking lot	унаа токтоочу жай	unaa toktootʃu dʒaj
subway	метро	metro
station	бекет	beket

to take the subway	метродо жүрүү	metrodo dʒyryy
train	поезд	poezd
train station	вокзал	vokzal

28. City. Life in the city

city, town	шаар	ʃaar
capital city	борбор	borbor
village	кыштак	kıʃtak

city map	шаардын планы	ʃaardın planı
downtown	шаардын борбору	ʃaardın borboru
suburb	шаардын чет жакасы	ʃaardın tʃet dʒakası
suburban (adj)	шаардын чет жакасындагы	ʃaardın tʃet dʒakasındagı

outskirts	чет-жака	tʃet-dʒaka
environs (suburbs)	чет-жака	tʃet-dʒaka
city block	квартал	kvartal
residential block (area)	турак-жай кварталы	turak-dʒaj kvartalı

traffic	көчө кыймылы	køtʃø kıjmılı
traffic lights	светофор	svetofor
public transportation	шаар транспорту	ʃaar transportu
intersection	кесилиш	kesiliʃ

crosswalk	жөө жүрүүчүлөр жолу	dʒøø dʒyryytʃylør dʒolu
pedestrian underpass	жер астындагы жол	dʒer astındagı dʒol
to cross (~ the street)	жолду өтүү	dʒoldu øtyy
pedestrian	жөө жүрүүчү	dʒøø dʒyryytʃy
sidewalk	жанжол	dʒandʒol

bridge	көпүрө	køpyrø
embankment (river walk)	жээк жол	dʒeek dʒol
fountain	фонтан	fontan

allée (garden walkway)	аллея	alleja
park	сейил багы	sejil bagı
boulevard	бульвар	bulʲvar
square	аянт	ajant
avenue (wide street)	проспект	prospekt
street	көчө	køtʃø
side street	чолок көчө	tʃolok køtʃø
dead end	туюк көчө	tujuk køtʃø

house	үй	yj
building	имарат	imarat
skyscraper	көк тиреген көп кабаттуу үй	køk tiregen køp kabattuu yj
facade	үйдүн алды	yjdyn aldı

roof	чатыр	tʃatır
window	терезе	tereze
arch	түркүк	tyrkyk
column	мамы	mamı
corner	бурч	burtʃ

store window	көрсөтмө айнек үкөк	kørsøtmø ajnek ykøk
signboard (store sign, etc.)	көрнөк	kørnøk
poster (e.g., playbill)	афиша	afiʃa
advertising poster	көрнөк-жарнак	kørnøk-dʒarnak
billboard	жарнамалык такта	dʒarnamalık takta

garbage, trash	таштанды	taʃtandı
trash can (public ~)	таштанды челек	taʃtandı tʃelek
to litter (vi)	таштоо	taʃtoo
garbage dump	таштанды үйүлгөн жер	taʃtandı yjylgøn dʒer

phone booth	телефон будкасы	telefon budkası
lamppost	чырак мамы	tʃırak mamı
bench (park ~)	отургуч	oturgutʃ

police officer	полиция кызматкери	politsija kızmatkeri
police	полиция	politsija
beggar	кайырчы	kajırtʃı
homeless (n)	селсаяк	selsajak

29. Urban institutions

store	дүкөн	dykøn
drugstore, pharmacy	дарыкана	darıkana
eyeglass store	оптика	optika
shopping mall	соода борбору	sooda borboru
supermarket	супермаркет	supermarket

bakery	нан дүкөнү	nan dykøny
baker	навайчы	navajtʃı
pastry shop	кондитердик дүкөн	konditerdik dykøn
grocery store	азык-түлүк	azık-tylyk
butcher shop	эт дүкөнү	et dykøny

| produce store | жашылча дүкөнү | dʒaʃıltʃa dykøny |
| market | базар | bazar |

coffee house	кофекана	kofekana
restaurant	ресторан	restoran
pub, bar	сыракана	sırakana
pizzeria	пиццерия	pitserija

| hair salon | чач тарач | tʃatʃ taratʃ |
| post office | почта | potʃta |

dry cleaners	химиялык тазалоо	χimijalık tazaloo
photo studio	фотоателье	fotoatelje
shoe store	бут кийим дүкөнү	but kijim dykøny
bookstore	китеп дүкөнү	kitep dykøny
sporting goods store	спорт буюмдар дүкөнү	sport bujɯmdar dykøny
clothes repair shop	кийим ондоочу жай	kijim ondootʃu dʒaj
formal wear rental	кийимди ижарага берүү	kijimdi idʒaraga beryy
video rental store	тасмаларды ижарага берүү	tasmalardı idʒaraga beryy
circus	цирк	tsırk
zoo	зоопарк	zoopark
movie theater	кинотеатр	kinoteatr
museum	музей	muzej
library	китепкана	kitepkana
theater	театр	teatr
opera (opera house)	опера	opera
nightclub	түнкү клуб	tynky klub
casino	казино	kazino
mosque	мечит	metʃit
synagogue	синагога	sinagoga
cathedral	чоң чиркөө	tʃoŋ tʃirkøø
temple	ибадаткана	ibadatkana
church	чиркөө	tʃirkøø
college	коллеж	kolledʒ
university	университет	universitet
school	мектеп	mektep
prefecture	префектура	prefektura
city hall	мэрия	merija
hotel	мейманкана	mejmankana
bank	банк	bank
embassy	элчилик	eltʃilik
travel agency	турагенттиги	turagenttigi
information office	маалымат бюросу	maalımat bɯrosu
currency exchange	алмаштыруу пункту	almaʃtıruu punktu
subway	метро	metro
hospital	оорукана	oorukana
gas station	май куюучу станция	maj kujɯutʃu stantsija
parking lot	унаа токтоочу жай	unaa toktootʃu dʒaj

30. Signs

signboard (store sign, etc.)	көрнөк	kørnøk
notice (door sign, etc.)	жазуу	dʒazuu
poster	көрнөк	kørnøk
direction sign	көрсөткүч	kørsøtkytʃ
arrow (sign)	жебе	dʒebe
caution	экертме	ekertme
warning sign	эскертүү белгиси	eskertyy belgisi
to warn (vt)	эскертүү	eskertyy
rest day (weekly ~)	дем алыш күн	dem alıʃ kyn
timetable (schedule)	ырааттама	ıraattama
opening hours	иш сааттары	iʃ saattarı
WELCOME!	КОШ КЕЛИҢИЗДЕР!	koʃ keliŋizder!
ENTRANCE	КИРҮҮ	kiryy
EXIT	ЧЫГУУ	tʃıguu
PUSH	ӨЗҮҢҮЗДӨН ТҮРТҮҢҮЗ	øzyŋyzdøn tyrtyŋyz
PULL	ӨЗҮҢҮЗГӨ ТАРТЫҢЫЗ	øzyŋyzgø tartıŋız
OPEN	АЧЫК	atʃık
CLOSED	ЖАБЫК	dʒabık
WOMEN	АЙЫМДАР ҮЧҮН	ajımdar ytʃyn
MEN	ЭРКЕКТЕР ҮЧҮН	erkekter ytʃyn
DISCOUNTS	АРЗАНДАТУУЛАР	arzandatuular
SALE	САТЫП ТҮГӨТҮҮ	satıp tygøtyy
NEW!	СААМАЛЫК!	saamalık!
FREE	БЕКЕР	beker
ATTENTION!	КӨҢҮЛ БУРУҢУЗ!	køŋyl buruŋuz!
NO VACANCIES	ОРУН ЖОК	orun dʒok
RESERVED	КАМДЫК БУЙРУТМАЛАГАН	kamdık bujrutmalagan
ADMINISTRATION	АДМИНИСТРАЦИЯ	administratsija
STAFF ONLY	ЖААМАТ ҮЧҮН ГАНА	dʒaamat ytʃyn gana
BEWARE OF THE DOG!	КАБАНААК ИТ	kabanaak it
NO SMOKING	ТАМЕКИ ЧЕГҮҮГӨ БОЛБОЙТ!	tameki tʃegyygø bolbojt!
DO NOT TOUCH!	КОЛУҢАР МЕНЕН КАРМАБАГЫЛА!	koluŋar menen karmabagıla!
DANGEROUS	КООПТУУ	kooptuu
DANGER	КОРКУНУЧ	korkunutʃ
HIGH VOLTAGE	ЖОГОРКУ ЧЫҢАЛУУ	dʒogorku tʃıŋaluu
NO SWIMMING!	СУУГА ТҮШҮҮГӨ БОЛБОЙТ	suuga tyʃyygø bolbojt

OUT OF ORDER	ИШТЕБЕЙТ	iʃtebejt
FLAMMABLE	ӨРТ ЧЫГУУ	ørt ʧiguu
	КОРКУНУЧУ	korkunuʧu
FORBIDDEN	ТЫЮУ САЛЫНГАН	tiɉu salıngan
NO TRESPASSING!	ӨТҮҮГӨ БОЛБОЙТ	øtyygø bolbojt
WET PAINT	СЫРДАЛГАН	sırdalgan

31. Shopping

to buy (purchase)	сатып алуу	satıp aluu
purchase	сатып алуу	satıp aluu
to go shopping	сатып алууга чыгуу	satıp aluuga ʧiguu
shopping	базарчылоо	bazarʧiloo

| to be open (ab. store) | иштөө | iʃtøø |
| to be closed | жабылуу | dʒabıluu |

footwear, shoes	бут кийим	but kijim
clothes, clothing	кийим-кече	kijim-keʧe
cosmetics	упа-эндик	upa-endik
food products	азык-түлүк	azık-tylyk
gift, present	белек	belek

| salesman | сатуучу | satuuʧu |
| saleswoman | сатуучу кыз | satuuʧu kız |

check out, cash desk	касса	kassa
mirror	күзгү	kyzgy
counter (store ~)	прилавок	prilavok
fitting room	кийим ченөөчү бөлмө	kijim ʧenøøʧy bølmø

to try on	кийим ченөө	kijim ʧenøø
to fit (ab. dress, etc.)	ылайык келүү	ılajık kelyy
to like (I like …)	жактыруу	dʒaktıruu

price	баа	baa
price tag	баа	baa
to cost (vt)	туруу	turuu
How much?	Канча?	kanʧa?
discount	арзандатуу	arzandatuu

inexpensive (adj)	кымбат эмес	kımbat emes
cheap (adj)	арзан	arzan
expensive (adj)	кымбат	kımbat
It's expensive	Бул кымбат	bul kımbat

rental (n)	ижара	idʒara
to rent (~ a tuxedo)	ижарага алуу	idʒaraga aluu
credit (trade credit)	насыя	nasıja
on credit (adv)	насыяга алуу	nasıjaga aluu

T&P BOOKS

CLOTHING & ACCESSORIES

T&P Books Publishing

clothes	кийим	kijim
outerwear	үстүңкү кийим	ystyŋky kijim
winter clothing	кышкы кийим	kıʃkı kijim

coat (overcoat)	пальто	palʲto
fur coat	тон	ton
fur jacket	чолок тон	tʃolok ton
down coat	мамык олпок	mamık olpok

jacket (e.g., leather ~)	күрмө	kyrmø
raincoat (trenchcoat, etc.)	плащ	plaʃtʃ
waterproof (adj)	суу өткүс	suu øtkys

shirt (button shirt)	көйнөк	køjnøk
pants	шым	ʃım
jeans	джинсы	dʒinsı
suit jacket	бешмант	beʃmant
suit	костюм	kostʉm

dress (frock)	көйнөк	køjnøk
skirt	юбка	jʉbka
blouse	блузка	bluzka
knitted jacket (cardigan, etc.)	кофта	kofta
jacket (of woman's suit)	кыска бешмант	kıska beʃmant

T-shirt	футболка	futbolka
shorts (short trousers)	чолок шым	tʃolok ʃım
tracksuit	спорт кийими	sport kijimi
bathrobe	халат	χalat
pajamas	пижама	pidʒama

sweater	свитер	sviter
pullover	пуловер	pulover

vest	жилет	dʒilet
tailcoat	фрак	frak
tuxedo	смокинг	smoking
uniform	форма	forma
workwear	жумуш кийим	dʒumuʃ kijim

| overalls | комбинезон | kombinezon |
| coat (e.g., doctor's smock) | халат | χalat |

34. Clothing. Underwear

underwear	ич кийим	itʃ kijim
boxers, briefs	эркектер чолок дамбалы	erkekter tʃolok dambalı
panties	аялдар трусиги	ajaldar trusigi
undershirt (A-shirt)	майка	majka
socks	байпак	bajpak
nightdress	жатаарда кийүүчү көйнөк	dʒataarda kijyytʃy køjnøk
bra	бюстгальтер	bʉstgalʲter
knee highs (knee-high socks)	гольфы	golʲfı
pantyhose	колготки	kolgotki
stockings (thigh highs)	байпак	bajpak
bathing suit	купальник	kupalʲnik

35. Headwear

hat	топу	topu
fedora	шляпа	ʃlʲapa
baseball cap	бейсболка	bejsbolka
flatcap	кепка	kepka
beret	берет	beret
hood	капюшон	kapʉʃon
panama hat	панамка	panamka
knit cap (knitted hat)	токулган шапка	tokulgan ʃapka
headscarf	жоолук	dʒooluk
women's hat	шляпа	ʃlʲapa
hard hat	каска	kaska
garrison cap	пилотка	pilotka
helmet	шлем	ʃlem
derby	котелок	kotelok
top hat	цилиндр	tsılindr

36. Footwear

| footwear | бут кийим | but kijim |
| shoes (men's shoes) | ботинка | botinka |

shoes (women's shoes)	туфли	tufli
boots (e.g., cowboy ~)	өтүк	øtyk
slippers	тапочка	tapotʃka

tennis shoes (e.g., Nike ~)	кроссовка	krossovka
sneakers	кеды	kedı
(e.g., Converse ~)		
sandals	сандалии	sandalii

cobbler (shoe repairer)	өтүкчү	øtyktʃy
heel	така	taka
pair (of shoes)	түгөй	tygøj

shoestring	боо	boo
to lace (vt)	боолоо	booloo
shoehorn	кашык	kaʃik
shoe polish	өтүк май	øtyk maj

37. Personal accessories

gloves	колкап	kolkap
mittens	мээлей	meelej
scarf (muffler)	моюн орогуч	mojʉn oroguʧ

glasses (eyeglasses)	көз айнек	køz ajnek
frame (eyeglass ~)	алкак	alkak
umbrella	чатырча	ʧatırʧa
walking stick	аса таяк	asa tajak

| hairbrush | тарак | tarak |
| fan | желпингич | dʒelpingiʧ |

| tie (necktie) | галстук | galstuk |
| bow tie | галстук-бабочка | galstuk-babotʃka |

| suspenders | шым тарткыч | ʃim tartkıʧ |
| handkerchief | бетаарчы | betaarʧı |

| comb | тарак | tarak |
| barrette | чачсайгы | ʧaʧsajgı |

| hairpin | шпилька | ʃpilʲka |
| buckle | таралга | taralga |

| belt | кайыш кур | kajıʃ kur |
| shoulder strap | илгич | ilgiʧ |

bag (handbag)	колбаштык	kolbaʃtık
purse	кичине колбаштык	kitʃine kolbaʃtık
backpack	жонбаштык	dʒonbaʃtık

38. Clothing. Miscellaneous

fashion	мода	moda
in vogue (adj)	саркеч	sarketʃ
fashion designer	модельер	modeljer

collar	жака	dʒaka
pocket	чөнтөк	tʃøntøk
pocket (as adj)	чөнтөк	tʃøntøk
sleeve	жең	dʒeŋ
hanging loop	илгич	ilgitʃ
fly (on trousers)	ширинка	ʃirinka

zipper (fastener)	молния	molnija
fastener	топчулук	toptʃuluk
button	топчу	toptʃu
buttonhole	илмек	ilmek
to come off (ab. button)	үзүлүү	yzylyy

to sew (vi, vt)	тигүү	tigyy
to embroider (vi, vt)	сайма саюу	sajma sajʉu
embroidery	сайма	sajma
sewing needle	ийне	ijne
thread	жип	dʒip
seam	тигиш	tigiʃ

to get dirty (vi)	булгап алуу	bulgap aluu
stain (mark, spot)	так	tak
to crease, crumple (vi)	бырышып калуу	bɪrɪʃɪp kaluu
to tear, to rip (vt)	айрылуу	ajrɪluu
clothes moth	күбө	kybø

39. Personal care. Cosmetics

toothpaste	тиш пастасы	tiʃ pastasɪ
toothbrush	тиш щёткасы	tiʃ ʃtʃʲotkasɪ
to brush one's teeth	тиш жуу	tiʃ dʒuu

razor	устара	ustara
shaving cream	кырынуу үчүн көбүк	kɪrɪnuu ytʃyn købyk
to shave (vi)	кырынуу	kɪrɪnuu

| soap | самын | samɪn |
| shampoo | шампунь | ʃampunʲ |

scissors	кайчы	kajtʃɪ
nail file	тырмак өгөө	tɪrmak øgøø
nail clippers	тырмак кычкачы	tɪrmak kɪtʃkatʃɪ
tweezers	искек	iskek

cosmetics	упа-эндик	upa-endik
face mask	маска	maska
manicure	маникюр	manikur
to have a manicure	маникюр жасоо	manikʤur ʤasoo
pedicure	педикюр	pedikur

make-up bag	косметичка	kosmetiʧka
face powder	упа	upa
powder compact	упа кутусу	upa kutusu
blusher	эндик	endik

perfume (bottled)	атыр	atır
toilet water (lotion)	туалет атыр суусу	tualet atır suusu
lotion	лосьон	losion
cologne	одеколон	odekolon

eyeshadow	көз боёгу	køz bojogu
eyeliner	көз карандашы	køz karandaʃı
mascara	кирпик үчүн боек	kirpik yʧyn boek

lipstick	эрин помадасы	erin pomadası
nail polish, enamel	тырмак үчүн лак	tırmak yʧyn lak
hair spray	чач үчүн лак	ʧaʧ yʧyn lak
deodorant	дезодорант	dezodorant

cream	крем	krem
face cream	бетмай	betmaj
hand cream	кол үчүн май	kol yʧyn maj
anti-wrinkle cream	бырыштарга каршы бет май	bırıʃtarga karʃı bet maj

day cream	күндүзгү бет май	kyndyzgy bet maj
night cream	түнкү бет май	tynky bet maj
day (as adj)	күндүзгү	kyndyzgy
night (as adj)	түнкү	tynky

tampon	тампон	tampon
toilet paper (toilet roll)	даарат кагазы	daarat kagazı
hair dryer	фен	fen

40. Watches. Clocks

watch (wristwatch)	кол саат	kol saat
dial	циферблат	tsıferblat
hand (of clock, watch)	жебе	ʤebe
metal watch band	браслет	braslet
watch strap	кайыш кур	kajıʃ kur

battery	батарейка	batarejka
to be dead (battery)	зарядканын түгөнүүсү	zariadkanın tygønyysy
to change a battery	батарейка алмаштыруу	batarejka almaʃtıruu

to run fast	алдыга кетүү	aldıga ketyy
to run slow	калуу	kaluu
wall clock	дубалга тагуучу саат	dubalga taguutʃu saat
hourglass	кум саат	kum saat
sundial	күн саат	kyn saat
alarm clock	ойготкуч саат	ojgotkutʃ saat
watchmaker	саат устасы	saat ustası
to repair (vt)	оңдоо	oŋdoo

EVERYDAY EXPERIENCE

T&P Books Publishing

41. Money

money	акча	akʧa
currency exchange	алмаштыруу	almaʃtıruu
exchange rate	курс	kurs
ATM	банкомат	bankomat
coin	тыйын	tıjın
dollar	доллар	dollar
euro	евро	evro
lira	италиялык лира	italijalık lira
Deutschmark	немис маркасы	nemis markası
franc	франк	frank
pound sterling	фунт стерлинг	funt sterling
yen	йена	jena
debt	карыз	karız
debtor	карыздар	karızdar
to lend (money)	карызга берүү	karızga beryy
to borrow (vi, vt)	карызга алуу	karızga aluu
bank	банк	bank
account	эсеп	esep
to deposit (vt)	салуу	saluu
to deposit into the account	эсепке акча салуу	esepke akʧa saluu
to withdraw (vt)	эсептен акча чыгаруу	esepten akʧa ʧıgaruu
credit card	насыя картасы	nasıja kartası
cash	накталай акча	naktalaj akʧa
check	чек	ʧek
to write a check	чек жазып берүү	ʧek dʒazıp beryy
checkbook	чек китепчеси	ʧek kitepʧesi
wallet	намыян	namıjan
change purse	капчык	kapʧık
safe	сейф	sejf
heir	мураскер	murasker
inheritance	мурас	muras
fortune (wealth)	мүлк	mylk
lease	ижара	idʒara
rent (money)	батир акысы	batir akısı
to rent (sth from sb)	батирге алуу	batirge aluu
price	баа	baa

cost	баа	baa
sum	сумма	summa
to spend (vi)	коротуу	korotuu
expenses	чыгым	tʃɩgɩm
to economize (vi, vt)	үнөмдөө	ynømdøø
economical	сарамжал	saramdʒal
to pay (vi, vt)	төлөө	tøløø
payment	акы төлөө	akɩ tøløø
change (give the ~)	кайтарылган майда акча	kajtarɩlgan majda aktʃa
tax	салык	salɩk
fine	айып	ajɩp
to fine (vt)	айып пул салуу	ajɩp pul saluu

42. Post. Postal service

post office	почта	potʃta
mail (letters, etc.)	почта	potʃta
mailman	кат ташуучу	kat taʃuutʃu
opening hours	иш сааттары	iʃ saattarɩ
letter	кат	kat
registered letter	тапшырык кат	tapʃɩrɩk kat
postcard	открытка	otkrɩtka
telegram	телеграмма	telegramma
package (parcel)	посылка	posɩlka
money transfer	акча которуу	aktʃa kotoruu
to receive (vt)	алуу	aluu
to send (vt)	жөнөтүү	dʒønøtyy
sending	жөнөтүү	dʒønøtyy
address	дарек	darek
ZIP code	индекс	indeks
sender	жөнөтүүчү	dʒønøtyytʃy
receiver	алуучу	aluutʃu
name (first name)	аты	atɩ
surname (last name)	фамилиясы	familijasɩ
postage rate	тариф	tarif
standard (adj)	жөнөкөй	dʒønøkøj
economical (adj)	үнөмдүү	ynømdyy
weight	салмак	salmak
to weigh (~ letters)	таразалоо	tarazaloo
envelope	конверт	konvert

| postage stamp | марка | marka |
| to stamp an envelope | марка жабыштыруу | marka dʒabıʃtıruu |

43. Banking

| bank | банк | bank |
| branch (of bank, etc.) | бөлүм | bølym |

| bank clerk, consultant | кеңешчи | keŋeʃʧi |
| manager (director) | башкаруучу | baʃkaruuʧu |

bank account	эсеп	esep
account number	эсеп номери	esep nomeri
checking account	учурдагы эсеп	uʧurdagı esep
savings account	топтолмо эсеп	toptolmo esep

| to open an account | эсеп ачуу | esep aʧuu |
| to close the account | эсеп жабуу | esep dʒabuu |

| to deposit into the account | эсепке акча салуу | esepke akʧa saluu |
| to withdraw (vt) | эсептен акча чыгаруу | esepten akʧa ʧıgaruu |

| deposit | аманат | amanat |
| to make a deposit | аманат кылуу | amanat kıluu |

| wire transfer | акча которуу | akʧa kotoruu |
| to wire, to transfer | акча которуу | akʧa kotoruu |

| sum | сумма | summa |
| How much? | Канча? | kanʧa? |

| signature | кол тамга | kol tamga |
| to sign (vt) | кол коюу | kol kojʉu |

| credit card | насыя картасы | nasıja kartası |
| code (PIN code) | код | kod |

| credit card number | насыя картанын номери | nasıja kartanın nomeri |
| ATM | банкомат | bankomat |

check	чек	ʧek
to write a check	чек жазып берүү	ʧek dʒazıp beryy
checkbook	чек китепчеси	ʧek kitepʧesi

loan (bank ~)	насыя	nasıja
to apply for a loan	насыя үчүн кайрылуу	nasıja yʧyn kajrıluu
to get a loan	насыя алуу	nasıja aluu
to give a loan	насыя берүү	nasıja beryy
guarantee	кепилдик	kepildik

44. Telephone. Phone conversation

telephone	телефон	telefon
cell phone	мобилдик	mobildik
answering machine	автоматтык жооп берүүчү	avtomattık dʒoop beryytʃy

to call (by phone)	чалуу	tʃaluu
phone call	чакыруу	tʃakıruu

to dial a number	номер терүү	nomer teryy
Hello!	Алло!	allo!
to ask (vt)	суроо	suroo
to answer (vi, vt)	жооп берүү	dʒoop beryy

to hear (vt)	угуу	uguu
well (adv)	жакшы	dʒakʃı
not well (adv)	жаман	dʒaman
noises (interference)	ызы-чуу	ızı-tʃuu

receiver	трубка	trubka
to pick up (~ the phone)	трубканы алуу	trubkanı aluu
to hang up (~ the phone)	трубканы коюу	trubkanı kojʉu

busy (engaged)	бош эмес	boʃ emes
to ring (ab. phone)	шыңгыроо	ʃıŋgıroo
telephone book	телефондук китепче	telefonduk kiteptʃe

local (adj)	жергиликтүү	dʒergiliktyy
local call	жергиликтүү чакыруу	dʒergiliktyy tʃakıruu
long distance (~ call)	шаар аралык	ʃaar aralık
long-distance call	шаар аралык чакыруу	ʃaar aralık tʃakıruu
international (adj)	эл аралык	el aralık
international call	эл аралык чакыруу	el aralık tʃakıruu

45. Cell phone

cell phone	мобилдик	mobildik
display	дисплей	displej
button	баскыч	baskıtʃ
SIM card	SIM-карта	sim-karta

battery	батарея	batareja
to be dead (battery)	зарядканын түгөнүүсү	zarʲadkanın tygønyysy
charger	заряддоочу шайман	zarʲaddootʃu ʃajman

menu	меню	menʉ
settings	орнотуулар	ornotuular
tune (melody)	обон	obon

to select (vt)	тандоо	tandoo
calculator	калькулятор	kalʲkulʲator
voice mail	автоматтык жооп бергич	avtomattık ʤoop bergitʃ

| alarm clock | ойготкуч | ojgotkutʃ |
| contacts | байланыштар | bajlanıʃtar |

| SMS (text message) | SMS-кабар | esemes-kabar |
| subscriber | абонент | abonent |

46. Stationery

| ballpoint pen | калем сап | kalem sap |
| fountain pen | калем уч | kalem utʃ |

pencil	карандаш	karandaʃ
highlighter	маркер	marker
felt-tip pen	фломастер	flomaster

| notepad | дептерче | deptertʃe |
| agenda (diary) | күндөлүк | kyndølyk |

ruler	сызгыч	sızgıtʃ
calculator	калькулятор	kalʲkulʲator
eraser	өчүргүч	øtʃyrgytʃ
thumbtack	кнопка	knopka
paper clip	кыскыч	kıskıtʃ

glue	желим	ʤelim
stapler	степлер	stepler
hole punch	тешкич	teʃkitʃ
pencil sharpener	учтагыч	utʃtagıtʃ

47. Foreign languages

language	тил	til
foreign (adj)	чет	tʃet
foreign language	чет тил	tʃet til
to study (vt)	окуу	okuu
to learn (language, etc.)	үйрөнүү	yjrønyy

to read (vi, vt)	окуу	okuu
to speak (vi, vt)	сүйлөө	syjløø
to understand (vt)	түшүнүү	tyʃynyy
to write (vt)	жазуу	ʤazuu

| fast (adv) | тез | tez |
| slowly (adv) | жай | ʤaj |

fluently (adv)	эркин	erkin
rules	эрежелер	eredʒeler
grammar	грамматика	grammatika
vocabulary	лексика	leksika
phonetics	фонетика	fonetika
textbook	китеп	kitep
dictionary	сөздүк	søzdyk
teach-yourself book	өзү үйрөткүч	øzy yjrøtkytʃ
phrasebook	тилачар	tilatʃar
cassette, tape	кассета	kasseta
videotape	видеокассета	videokasseta
CD, compact disc	CD, компакт-диск	sidi, kompakt-disk
DVD	DVD-диск	dividi-disk
alphabet	алфавит	alfavit
to spell (vt)	эжелеп айтуу	edʒelep ajtuu
pronunciation	айтылышы	ajtılıʃı
accent	акцент	aktsent
with an accent	акцент менен	aktsent menen
without an accent	акцентсиз	aktsentsiz
word	сөз	søz
meaning	маани	maani
course (e.g., a French ~)	курстар	kurstar
to sign up	курска жазылуу	kurska dʒazıluu
teacher	окутуучу	okutuutʃu
translation (process)	которуу	kotoruu
translation (text, etc.)	котормо	kotormo
translator	котормочу	kotormotʃu
interpreter	оозеки котормочу	oozeki kotormotʃu
polyglot	полиглот	poliglot
memory	эс тутум	es tutum

MEALS. RESTAURANT

T&P Books Publishing

48. Table setting

spoon	кашык	kaʃık
knife	бычак	bɪʧak
fork	вилка	vilka

cup (e.g., coffee ~)	чөйчөк	ʧøjʧøk
plate (dinner ~)	табак	tabak
saucer	табак	tabak

| napkin (on table) | майлык | majlık |
| toothpick | тиш чукугуч | tiʃ ʧukuguʧ |

49. Restaurant

| restaurant | ресторан | restoran |
| coffee house | кофекана | kofekana |

| pub, bar | бар | bar |
| tearoom | чай салону | ʧaj salonu |

waiter	официант	ofitsiant
waitress	официант кыз	ofitsiant kız
bartender	бармен	barmen

menu	меню	menʉ
wine list	шарап картасы	ʃarap kartası
to book a table	столду камдык буйрутмалоо	stoldu kamdık bujrutmaloo

course, dish	тамак	tamak
to order (meal)	буйрутма кылуу	bujrutma kıluu
to make an order	буйрутма берүү	bujrutma beryy

aperitif	аперитив	aperitiv
appetizer	ысылык	ısılık
dessert	десерт	desert

| check | эсеп | esep |
| to pay the check | эсеп төлөө | esep tøløø |

| to give change | майда акчаны кайтаруу | majda akʧanı kajtaruu |
| tip | чайпул | ʧajpul |

50. Meals

food	тамак	tamak
to eat (vi, vt)	тамактануу	tamaktanuu
breakfast	таңкы тамак	taŋkı tamak
to have breakfast	эртең менен	erteŋ menen
	тамактануу	tamaktanuu
lunch	түшкү тамак	tyʃky tamak
to have lunch	түштөнүү	tyʃtønyy
dinner	кечки тамак	ketʃki tamak
to have dinner	кечки тамакты ичүү	ketʃki tamaktı itʃyy
appetite	табит	tabit
Enjoy your meal!	Тамагыңыз таттуу	tamagıŋız tattuu
	болсун!	bolsun!
to open (~ a bottle)	ачуу	atʃuu
to spill (liquid)	төгүп алуу	tøgyp aluu
to spill out (vi)	төгүлүү	tøgylyy
to boil (vi)	кайноо	kajnoo
to boil (vt)	кайнатуу	kajnatuu
boiled (~ water)	кайнатылган	kajnatılgan
to chill, cool down (vt)	суутуу	suutuu
to chill (vi)	сууп туруу	suup turuu
taste, flavor	даам	daam
aftertaste	даамдануу	daamdanuu
to slim down (lose weight)	арыктоо	arıktoo
diet	мүнөз тамак	mynøz tamak
vitamin	витамин	vitamin
calorie	калория	kalorija
vegetarian (n)	эттен чанган	etten tʃangan
vegetarian (adj)	этсиз даярдалган	etsiz dajardalgan
fats (nutrient)	майлар	majlar
proteins	белоктор	beloktor
carbohydrates	көмүрсуулар	kømyrsuular
slice (of lemon, ham)	кесим	kesim
piece (of cake, pie)	бөлүк	bølyk
crumb	күкүм	kykym
(of bread, cake, etc.)		

51. Cooked dishes

course, dish	тамак	tamak
cuisine	даам	daam

recipe	тамак жасоо ыкмасы	tamak dʒasoo ıkması
portion	порция	portsija
salad	салат	salat
soup	сорпо	sorpo
clear soup (broth)	ынак сорпо	ınak sorpo
sandwich (bread)	бутерброд	buterbrod
fried eggs	куурулган жумуртка	kuurulgan dʒumurtka
hamburger (beefburger)	гамбургер	gamburger
beefsteak	бифштекс	bifʃteks
side dish	гарнир	garnir
spaghetti	спагетти	spagetti
mashed potatoes	эзилген картошка	ezilgen kartoʃka
pizza	пицца	pitsa
porridge (oatmeal, etc.)	ботко	botko
omelet	омлет	omlet
boiled (e.g., ~ beef)	сууга бышырылган	suuga bıʃırılgan
smoked (adj)	ышталган	ıʃtalgan
fried (adj)	куурулган	kuurulgan
dried (adj)	кургатылган	kurgatılgan
frozen (adj)	тоңдурулган	toŋdurulgan
pickled (adj)	маринаддагы	marinaddagı
sweet (sugary)	таттуу	tattuu
salty (adj)	туздуу	tuzduu
cold (adj)	муздак	muzdak
hot (adj)	ысык	ısık
bitter (adj)	ачуу	atʃuu
tasty (adj)	даамдуу	daamduu
to cook in boiling water	кайнатуу	kajnatuu
to cook (dinner)	тамак бышыруу	tamak bıʃıruu
to fry (vt)	кууруу	kuuruu
to heat up (food)	жылытуу	dʒılıtuu
to salt (vt)	туздоо	tuzdoo
to pepper (vt)	калемпир кошуу	kalempir koʃuu
to grate (vt)	сүргүлөө	syrgyløø
peel (n)	сырты	sırtı
to peel (vt)	тазалоо	tazaloo

52. Food

meat	эт	et
chicken	тоок	took
Rock Cornish hen (poussin)	балапан	balapan

duck	өрдөк	ørdøk
goose	каз	kaz
game	илбээсин	ilbeesin
turkey	күрп	kyrp

pork	чочко эти	t∫ot∫ko eti
veal	торпок эти	torpok eti
lamb	кой эти	koj eti
beef	уй эти	uj eti
rabbit	коен	koen

sausage (bologna, etc.)	колбаса	kolbasa
vienna sausage (frankfurter)	сосиска	sosiska
bacon	бекон	bekon
ham	ветчина	vett∫ina
gammon	сан эт	san et

pâté	паштет	pa∫tet
liver	боор	boor
hamburger (ground beef)	фарш	far∫
tongue	тил	til

egg	жумуртка	dʒumurtka
eggs	жумурткалар	dʒumurtkalar
egg white	жумуртканын агы	dʒumurtkanın agı
egg yolk	жумуртканын сарысы	dʒumurtkanın sarısı

fish	балык	balık
seafood	деңиз азыктары	deŋiz azıktarı
crustaceans	рак сыяктуулар	rak sıjaktuular
caviar	урук	uruk

crab	краб	krab
shrimp	креветка	krevetka
oyster	устрица	ustrit∫a
spiny lobster	лангуст	langust
octopus	сегиз бут	segiz but
squid	кальмар	kalʲmar

sturgeon	осетрина	osetrina
salmon	лосось	lososʲ
halibut	палтус	paltus

cod	треска	treska
mackerel	скумбрия	skumbrija
tuna	тунец	tunet∫
eel	угорь	ugorʲ

trout	форель	forelʲ
sardine	сардина	sardina
pike	чортон	t∫orton

herring	сельдь	selʲdʲ
bread	нан	nan
cheese	сыр	sır
sugar	кум шекер	kum-ʃeker
salt	туз	tuz

rice	күрүч	kyrytʃ
pasta (macaroni)	макарон	makaron
noodles	кесме	kesme

butter	ак май	ak maj
vegetable oil	өсүмдүк майы	øsymdyk majı
sunflower oil	күн карама майы	kyn karama majı
margarine	маргарин	margarin

olives	зайтун	zajtun
olive oil	зайтун майы	zajtun majı

milk	сүт	syt
condensed milk	коютулган сүт	kojʉtulgan syt
yogurt	йогурт	jogurt
sour cream	сметана	smetana
cream (of milk)	каймак	kajmak

mayonnaise	майонез	majonez
buttercream	крем	krem

groats (barley ~, etc.)	акшак	akʃak
flour	ун	un
canned food	консерва	konserva

cornflakes	жарылган жүгөрү	dʒarılgan dʒygøry
honey	бал	bal
jam	джем, конфитюр	dʒem, konfitʉr
chewing gum	сагыз	sagız

53. Drinks

water	суу	suu
drinking water	ичүүчү суу	itʃyytʃy suu
mineral water	минерал суусу	mineral suusu

still (adj)	газсыз	gazsız
carbonated (adj)	газдалган	gazdalgan
sparkling (adj)	газы менен	gazı menen
ice	муз	muz
with ice	музу менен	muzu menen

non-alcoholic (adj)	алкоголсуз	alkogolsuz
soft drink	алкоголсуз ичимдик	alkogolsuz itʃimdik

refreshing drink	суусундук	suusunduk
lemonade	лимонад	limonad

liquors	спирт ичимдиктери	spirt itʃimdikteri
wine	шарап	ʃarap
white wine	ак шарап	ak ʃarap
red wine	кызыл шарап	kızıl ʃarap

liqueur	ликёр	likʲor
champagne	шампан	ʃampan
vermouth	вермут	vermut

whiskey	виски	viski
vodka	арак	arak
gin	джин	dʒin
cognac	коньяк	konjak
rum	ром	rom

coffee	кофе	kofe
black coffee	кара кофе	kara kofe
coffee with milk	сүттөлгөн кофе	syttølgøn kofe
cappuccino	капучино	kaputʃino
instant coffee	эрүүчү кофе	eryytʃy kofe

milk	сүт	syt
cocktail	коктейль	koktejlʲ
milkshake	сүт коктейли	syt koktejli

juice	шире	ʃire
tomato juice	томат ширеси	tomat ʃiresi
orange juice	апельсин ширеси	apelʲsin ʃiresi
freshly squeezed juice	түз сыгылып алынган шире	tyz sıgılıp alıngan ʃire

beer	сыра	sıra
light beer	ачык сыра	atʃık sıra
dark beer	коңур сыра	koŋur sıra

tea	чай	tʃaj
black tea	кара чай	kara tʃaj
green tea	жашыл чай	dʒaʃıl tʃaj

54. Vegetables

vegetables	жашылча	dʒaʃıltʃa
greens	көк чөп	køk tʃøp

tomato	помидор	pomidor
cucumber	бадыраң	badıraŋ
carrot	сабиз	sabiz

potato	картошка	kartoʃka
onion	пияз	pijaz
garlic	сарымсак	sarımsak

cabbage	капуста	kapusta
cauliflower	гүлдүү капуста	gyldyy kapusta
Brussels sprouts	брюссель капустасы	brʉsselʲ kapustası
broccoli	брокколи капустасы	brokkoli kapustası

beet	кызылча	kızıltʃa
eggplant	баклажан	bakladʒan
zucchini	кабачок	kabatʃok
pumpkin	ашкабак	aʃkabak
turnip	шалгам	ʃalgam

parsley	петрушка	petruʃka
dill	укроп	ukrop
lettuce	салат	salat
celery	сельдерей	selʲderej
asparagus	спаржа	spardʒa
spinach	шпинат	ʃpinat

pea	нокот	nokot
beans	буурчак	buurtʃak
corn (maize)	жүгөрү	dʒygøry
kidney bean	төө буурчак	tøø buurtʃak

bell pepper	таттуу перец	tattuu perets
radish	шалгам	ʃalgam
artichoke	артишок	artiʃok

55. Fruits. Nuts

fruit	мөмө	mømø
apple	алма	alma
pear	алмурут	almurut
lemon	лимон	limon
orange	апельсин	apelʲsin
strawberry (garden ~)	кулпунай	kulpunaj

mandarin	мандарин	mandarin
plum	кара өрүк	kara øryk
peach	шабдаалы	ʃabdaalı
apricot	өрүк	øryk
raspberry	дан куурай	dan kuuraj
pineapple	ананас	ananas

banana	банан	banan
watermelon	арбуз	arbuz
grape	жүзүм	dʒyzym

sour cherry	алча	alʧa
sweet cherry	гилас	gilas
melon	коон	koon

grapefruit	грейпфрут	grejpfrut
avocado	авокадо	avokado
papaya	папайя	papaja
mango	манго	mango
pomegranate	анар	anar

redcurrant	кызыл карагат	kızıl karagat
blackcurrant	кара карагат	kara karagat
gooseberry	крыжовник	krıdʒovnik
bilberry	кара моюл	kara mojul
blackberry	кара бүлдүркөн	kara byldyrkøn

raisin	мейиз	mejiz
fig	анжир	andʒir
date	курма	kurma

peanut	арахис	araχis
almond	бадам	badam
walnut	жаңгак	dʒaŋgak
hazelnut	токой жаңгагы	tokoj dʒaŋgagı
coconut	кокос жаңгагы	kokos dʒaŋgagı
pistachios	мисте	miste

56. Bread. Candy

bakers' confectionery (pastry)	кондитер азыктары	konditer azıktarı
bread	нан	nan
cookies	печенье	petʃenje

chocolate (n)	шоколад	ʃokolad
chocolate (as adj)	шоколаддан	ʃokoladdan
candy (wrapped)	конфета	konfeta

| cake (e.g., cupcake) | пирожное | pirodʒnoe |
| cake (e.g., birthday ~) | торт | tort |

| pie (e.g., apple ~) | пирог | pirog |
| filling (for cake, pie) | начинка | natʃinka |

| jam (whole fruit jam) | кыям | kıjam |
| marmalade | мармелад | marmelad |

wafers	вафли	vafli
ice-cream	бал муздак	bal muzdak
pudding	пудинг	puding

57. Spices

salt	туз	tuz
salty (adj)	туздуу	tuzduu
to salt (vt)	туздоо	tuzdoo
black pepper	кара мурч	kara murtʃ
red pepper (milled ~)	кызыл калемпир	kızıl kalempir
mustard	горчица	gortʃitsa
horseradish	хрен	χren
condiment	татымал	tatımal
spice	татымал	tatımal
sauce	соус	sous
vinegar	уксус	uksus
anise	анис	anis
basil	райхон	rajχon
cloves	гвоздика	gvozdika
ginger	имбирь	imbirʲ
coriander	кориандр	koriandr
cinnamon	корица	koritsa
sesame	кунжут	kundʒut
bay leaf	лавр жалбырагы	lavr dʒalbıragı
paprika	паприка	paprika
caraway	зира	zira
saffron	заапаран	zaaparan

T&P BOOKS

PERSONAL INFORMATION. FAMILY

T&P Books Publishing

58. Personal information. Forms

name (first name)	аты	atı
surname (last name)	фамилиясы	familijası
date of birth	төрөлгөн күнү	tørølgøn kyny
place of birth	туулган жери	tuulgan dʒeri
nationality	улуту	ulutu
place of residence	жашаган жери	dʒaʃagan dʒeri
country	өлкө	ølkø
profession (occupation)	кесиби	kesibi
gender, sex	жынысы	dʒınısı
height	бою	boju
weight	салмак	salmak

59. Family members. Relatives

mother	эне	ene
father	ата	ata
son	уул	uul
daughter	кыз	kız
younger daughter	кичүү кыз	kitʃyy kız
younger son	кичүү уул	kitʃyy uul
eldest daughter	улуу кыз	uluu kız
eldest son	улуу уул	uluu uul
brother	бир тууган	bir tuugan
elder brother	байке	bajke
younger brother	ини	ini
sister	бир тууган	bir tuugan
elder sister	эже	edʒe
younger sister	синди	siŋdi
cousin (masc.)	атасы же энеси бир тууган	atası dʒe enesi bir tuugan
cousin (fem.)	атасы же энеси бир тууган	atası dʒe enesi bir tuugan
mom, mommy	апа	apa
dad, daddy	ата	ata
parents	ата-эне	ata-ene
child	бала	bala

children	балдар	baldar
grandmother	чоң апа	tʃoŋ apa
grandfather	чоң ата	tʃoŋ ata
grandson	небере бала	nebere bala
granddaughter	небере кыз	nebere kız
grandchildren	небврелер	nebereler

uncle	таяке	tajake
aunt	таяже	tajadʒe
nephew	ини	ini
niece	жээн	dʒeen

mother-in-law (wife's mother)	кайын эне	kajın ene
father-in-law (husband's father)	кайын ата	kajın ata
son-in-law (daughter's husband)	күйөө бала	kyjøø bala
stepmother	өгөй эне	øgøj ene
stepfather	өгөй ата	øgøj ata

infant	эмчектеги бала	emtʃektegi bala
baby (infant)	ымыркай	ımırkaj
little boy, kid	бөбөк	bøbøk

wife	аял	ajal
husband	эр	er

spouse (husband)	күйөө	kyjøø
spouse (wife)	зайып	zajıp

married (masc.)	аялы бар	ajalı bar
married (fem.)	күйөөдө	kyjøødø
single (unmarried)	бойдок	bojdok
bachelor	бойдок	bojdok
divorced (masc.)	ажырашкан	adʒıraʃkan

widow	жесир	dʒesir
widower	жесир	dʒesir

relative	тууган	tuugan
close relative	жакын тууган	dʒakın tuugan

distant relative	алыс тууган	alıs tuugan
relatives	бир тууган	bir tuugan

orphan (boy or girl)	жетим	dʒetim
guardian (of a minor)	камкорчу	kamkortʃu
to adopt (a boy)	уул кылып асырап алуу	uul kılıp asırap aluu
to adopt (a girl)	кыз кылып асырап алуу	kız kılıp asırap aluu

60. Friends. Coworkers

friend (masc.)	дос	dos
friend (fem.)	курбу	kurbu
friendship	достук	dostuk
to be friends	достошуу	dostoʃuu
buddy (masc.)	шерик	ʃerik
buddy (fem.)	шерик кыз	ʃerik kız
partner	өнөктөш	ønøktøʃ
chief (boss)	башчы	baʃʧı
superior (n)	башчы	baʃʧı
owner, proprietor	кожоюн	kodʒodʒʉn
subordinate (n)	кол астындагы	kol astındagı
colleague	кесиптеш	kesipteʃ
acquaintance (person)	тааныш	taanıʃ
fellow traveler	жолдош	dʒoldoʃ
classmate	классташ	klasstaʃ
neighbor (masc.)	кошуна	koʃuna
neighbor (fem.)	кошуна	koʃuna
neighbors	кошуналар	koʃunalar

HUMAN BODY.
MEDICINE

T&P Books Publishing

61. Head

head	баш	baʃ
face	бет	bet
nose	мурун	murun
mouth	ооз	ooz
eye	көз	køz
eyes	көздөр	køzdør
pupil	карек	karek
eyebrow	каш	kaʃ
eyelash	кирпик	kirpik
eyelid	кабак	kabak
tongue	тил	til
tooth	тиш	tiʃ
lips	эриндер	erinder
cheekbones	бет сөөгү	bet søøgy
gum	тиш эти	tiʃ eti
palate	таңдай	taŋdaj
nostrils	мурун тешиги	murun teʃigi
chin	ээк	eek
jaw	жаак	dʒaak
cheek	бет	bet
forehead	чеке	tʃeke
temple	чыкый	tʃɪkɪj
ear	кулак	kulak
back of the head	желке	dʒelke
neck	моюн	mojʉn
throat	тамак	tamak
hair	чач	tʃatʃ
hairstyle	чач жасоо	tʃatʃ dʒasoo
haircut	чач кыркуу	tʃatʃ kɪrkuu
wig	парик	parik
mustache	мурут	murut
beard	сакал	sakal
to have (a beard, etc.)	мурут коюу	murut kojʉu
braid	өрүм чач	ørym tʃatʃ
sideburns	бакенбарда	bakenbarda
red-haired (adj)	сары	sarı
gray (hair)	ак чачтуу	ak tʃatʃtuu

| bald (adj) | таз | taz |
| bald patch | кашка | kaʃka |

| ponytail | куйрук | kujruk |
| bangs | көкүл | køkyl |

62. Human body

| hand | беш манжа | beʃ manʤa |
| arm | кол | kol |

finger	манжа	manʤa
toe	манжа	manʤa
thumb	бармак	barmak
little finger	чыпалак	tʃɪpalak
nail	тырмак	tɪrmak

fist	муштум	muʃtum
palm	алакан	alakan
wrist	билек	bilek
forearm	каруу	karuu
elbow	чыканак	tʃɪkanak
shoulder	ийин	ijin

leg	бут	but
foot	таман	taman
knee	тизе	tize
calf (part of leg)	балтыр	baltɪr
hip	сан	san
heel	согончок	sogontʃok

body	дене	dene
stomach	курсак	kursak
chest	төш	tøʃ
breast	эмчек	emtʃek
flank	каптал	kaptal
back	арка жон	arka ʤon

| lower back | бел | bel |
| waist | бел | bel |

navel (belly button)	киндик	kindik
buttocks	жамбаш	ʤambaʃ
bottom	көчүк	køtʃyk

beauty mark	мең	meŋ
birthmark	кал	kal
(café au lait spot)		
tattoo	татуировка	tatuirovka
scar	тырык	tɪrɪk

63. Diseases

sickness	оору	ooru
to be sick	ооруу	ooruu
health	ден-соолук	den-sooluk

runny nose (coryza)	мурдунан суу агуу	murdunan suu aguu
tonsillitis	ангина	angina
cold (illness)	суук тийүү	suuk tijyy
to catch a cold	суук тийгизип алуу	suuk tijgizip aluu

bronchitis	бронхит	bronχit
pneumonia	кабыргадан сезгенүү	kabırgadan sezgenyy
flu, influenza	сасык тумоо	sasık tumoo

nearsighted (adj)	алыстан көрө албоо	alıstan kørø alboo
farsighted (adj)	жакындан көрө албоо	dʒakından kørø alboo
strabismus (crossed eyes)	кылый көздүүлүк	kılıj køzdyylyk
cross-eyed (adj)	кылый көздүүлүк	kılıj køzdyylyk
cataract	челкөз	tʃelkøz
glaucoma	глаукома	glaukoma

stroke	мээге кан куюлуу	meege kan kujuluu
heart attack	инфаркт	infarkt
myocardial infarction	инфаркт миокарда	infarkt miokarda
paralysis	шал	ʃal
to paralyze (vt)	шал болуу	ʃal boluu

allergy	аллергия	allergija
asthma	астма	astma
diabetes	диабет	diabet

toothache	тиш оорусу	tiʃ oorusu
caries	кариес	karies

diarrhea	ич өткү	itʃ øtky
constipation	ич катуу	itʃ katuu
stomach upset	ич бузулгандык	itʃ buzulgandık
food poisoning	уулануу	uulanuu
to get food poisoning	уулануу	uulanuu

arthritis	артрит	artrit
rickets	итий	itij
rheumatism	кызыл жүгүрүк	kızıl dʒygyryk
atherosclerosis	атеросклероз	ateroskleroz

gastritis	карын сезгенүүсу	karın sezgenyysu
appendicitis	аппендицит	appenditsit
cholecystitis	холецистит	χoletsistit
ulcer	жара	dʒara
measles	кызылча	kızıltʃa

rubella (German measles)	кызамык	kızamık
jaundice	сарык	sarık
hepatitis	гепатит	gepatit

schizophrenia	шизофрения	ʃizofrenija
rabies (hydrophobia)	кутурма	kuturma
neurosis	невроз	nevroz
concussion	мээнин чайкалышы	meenin tʃajkalıʃı

cancer	рак	rak
sclerosis	склероз	skleroz
multiple sclerosis	жайылган склероз	dʒajılgan skleroz

alcoholism	аракечтик	araketʃtik
alcoholic (n)	аракеч	araketʃ
syphilis	котон жара	koton dʒara
AIDS	СПИД	spid

tumor	шишик	ʃiʃik
malignant (adj)	залалдуу	zalalduu
benign (adj)	залалсыз	zalalsız

fever	безгек	bezgek
malaria	безгек	bezgek
gangrene	кабыз	kabız
seasickness	деңиз оорусу	deŋiz oorusu
epilepsy	талма	talma

epidemic	эпидемия	epidemija
typhus	келте	kelte
tuberculosis	кургак учук	kurgak utʃuk
cholera	холера	χolera
plague (bubonic ~)	кара тумоо	kara tumoo

64. Symptoms. Treatments. Part 1

symptom	белги	belgi
temperature	дене табынын көтөрүлүшү	dene tabının køtørylyʃy
high temperature (fever)	жогорку температура	dʒogorku temperatura
pulse (heartbeat)	тамыр кагышы	tamır kagıʃı

dizziness (vertigo)	баш айлануу	baʃ ajlanuu
hot (adj)	ысык	ısık
shivering	чыйрыгуу	tʃıjrıguu
pale (e.g., ~ face)	купкуу	kupkuu

cough	жөтөл	dʒøtøl
to cough (vi)	жөтөлүү	dʒøtølyy
to sneeze (vi)	чүчкүрүү	tʃytʃkyryy

| faint | эси оо | esi oo |
| to faint (vi) | эси ооп жыгылуу | esi oop dʒıgıluu |

bruise (hématome)	көк-ала	køk-ala
bump (lump)	шишик	ʃiʃik
to bang (bump)	урунуп алуу	urunup aluu
contusion (bruise)	көгөртүп алуу	køgørtyp aluu
to get a bruise	көгөртүп алуу	køgørtyp aluu

to limp (vi)	аксоо	aksoo
dislocation	муундун чыгып кетүүсү	muundun tʃıgıp ketyysy
to dislocate (vt)	чыгарып алуу	tʃıgarıp aluu
fracture	сынуу	sınuu
to have a fracture	сындырып алуу	sındırıp aluu

cut (e.g., paper ~)	кесилген жер	kesilgen dʒer
to cut oneself	кесип алуу	kesip aluu
bleeding	кан кетүү	kan ketyy

| burn (injury) | күйүк | kyjyk |
| to get burned | күйгүзүп алуу | kyjgyzyp aluu |

to prick (vt)	саюу	sajʉu
to prick oneself	сайып алуу	sajıp aluu
to injure (vt)	кокустатып алуу	kokustatıp aluu
injury	кокустатып алуу	kokustatıp aluu
wound	жара	dʒara
trauma	жаракат	dʒarakat

to be delirious	жөлүү	dʒølyy
to stutter (vi)	кекечтенүү	keketʃtenyy
sunstroke	күн өтүү	kyn øtyy

65. Symptoms. Treatments. Part 2

| pain, ache | оору | ooru |
| splinter (in foot, etc.) | тикен | tiken |

sweat (perspiration)	тер	ter
to sweat (perspire)	тердөө	terdøø
vomiting	кусуу	kusuu
convulsions	тарамыш карышуусу	taramıʃ karıʃuusu

pregnant (adj)	кош бойлуу	koʃ bojluu
to be born	төрөлүү	tørølyy
delivery, labor	төрөт	tørøt
to deliver (~ a baby)	төрөө	tørøø
abortion	бойдон түшүрүү	bojdon tyʃyryy
breathing, respiration	дем алуу	dem aluu
in-breath (inhalation)	дем алуу	dem aluu

out-breath (exhalation)	дем чыгаруу	dem tʃɪgaruu
to exhale (breathe out)	дем чыгаруу	dem tʃɪgaruu
to inhale (vi)	дем алуу	dem aluu
disabled person	майып	majɪp
cripple	мунжу	mundʒu
drug addict	баңги	baŋgi
deaf (adj)	дүлөй	dyløj
mute (adj)	дудук	duduk
deaf mute (adj)	дудук	duduk
mad, insane (adj)	жин тийген	dʒin tijgen
madman	жинди чалыш	dʒindi tʃalɪʃ
(demented person)		
madwoman	жинди чалыш	dʒindi tʃalɪʃ
to go insane	мээси айныган	meesi ajnɪgan
gene	ген	gen
immunity	иммунитет	immunitet
hereditary (adj)	тукум куучулук	tukum kuutʃuluk
congenital (adj)	тубаса	tubasa
virus	вирус	virus
microbe	микроб	mikrob
bacterium	бактерия	bakterija
infection	жугуштуу илдет	dʒuguʃtuu ildet

66. Symptoms. Treatments. Part 3

hospital	оорукана	oorukana
patient	бейтап	bejtap
diagnosis	дарт аныктоо	dart anɪktoo
cure	дарылоо	darɪloo
medical treatment	дарылоо	darɪloo
to get treatment	дарылануу	darɪlanuu
to treat (~ a patient)	дарылоо	darɪloo
to nurse (look after)	кароо	karoo
care (nursing ~)	кароо	karoo
operation, surgery	операция	operatsija
to bandage (head, limb)	жараны таңуу	dʒaranɪ taŋuu
bandaging	таңуу	taŋuu
vaccination	эмдөө	emdøø
to vaccinate (vt)	эмдөө	emdøø
injection, shot	ийне салуу	ijne saluu
to give an injection	ийне сайдыруу	ijne sajdɪruu
attack	оору кармап калуу	ooru karmap kaluu

amputation	кесүү	kesyy
to amputate (vt)	кесип таштоо	kesip taʃtoo
coma	кома	koma
to be in a coma	комада болуу	komada boluu
intensive care	реанимация	reanimatsija
to recover (~ from flu)	сакаюу	sakajɰu
condition (patient's ~)	абал	abal
consciousness	эсинде	esinde
memory (faculty)	эс тутум	es tutum
to pull out (tooth)	тишти жулуу	tiʃti dʒuluu
filling	пломба	plomba
to fill (a tooth)	пломба салуу	plomba saluu
hypnosis	гипноз	gipnoz
to hypnotize (vt)	гипноз кылуу	gipnoz kıluu

67. Medicine. Drugs. Accessories

medicine, drug	дары-дармек	darı-darmek
remedy	дары	darı
to prescribe (vt)	жазып берүү	dʒazıp beryy
prescription	рецепт	retsept
tablet, pill	таблетка	tabletka
ointment	май	maj
ampule	ампула	ampula
mixture, solution	аралашма	aralaʃma
syrup	сироп	sirop
capsule	пилюля	pilɰlʲa
powder	күкүм	kykym
gauze bandage	бинт	bint
cotton wool	пахта	paxta
iodine	йод	jod
Band-Aid	лейкопластырь	lejkoplastırʲ
eyedropper	дары тамызгыч	darı tamızgıtʃ
thermometer	градусник	gradusnik
syringe	шприц	ʃprits
wheelchair	майып арабасы	majıp arabası
crutches	колтук таяк	koltuk tajak
painkiller	оору сездирбөөчү дары	ooru sezdirbøøtʃy darı
laxative	ич алдыруучу дары	itʃ aldıruutʃu darı
spirits (ethanol)	спирт	spirt
medicinal herbs	дары чөптөр	darı tʃøptør
herbal (~ tea)	чөп чайы	tʃøp tʃajı

APARTMENT

T&P Books Publishing

68. Apartment

apartment	батир	batir
room	бөлмө	bølmø
bedroom	уктоочу бөлмө	uktootʃu bølmø
dining room	ашкана	aʃkana
living room	конок үйү	konok yjy
study (home office)	иш бөлмөсү	iʃ bølmøsy
entry room	кире бериш	kire beriʃ
bathroom (room with a bath or shower)	ванная	vannaja
half bath	даараткана	daaratkana
ceiling	шып	ʃɪp
floor	пол	pol
corner	бурч	burtʃ

69. Furniture. Interior

furniture	эмерек	emerek
table	стол	stol
chair	стул	stul
bed	керебет	kerebet
couch, sofa	диван	divan
armchair	олпок отургуч	olpok oturgutʃ
bookcase	китеп шкафы	kitep ʃkafɪ
shelf	текче	tektʃe
wardrobe	шкаф	ʃkaf
coat rack (wall-mounted ~)	кийим илгич	kijim ilgitʃ
coat stand	кийим илгич	kijim ilgitʃ
bureau, dresser	комод	komod
coffee table	журнал столу	dʒurnal stolu
mirror	күзгү	kyzgy
carpet	килем	kilem
rug, small carpet	килемче	kilemtʃe
fireplace	очок	otʃok
candle	шам	ʃam
candlestick	шамдал	ʃamdal

drapes	парда	parda
wallpaper	туш кагаз	tuʃ kagaz
blinds (jalousie)	жалюзи	dʒaldʒʉzi

table lamp	стол чырагы	stol tʃɪragɪ
wall lamp (sconce)	чырак	tʃɪrak
floor lamp	торшер	torʃer
chandelier	асма шам	asma ʃam

leg (of chair, table)	бут	but
armrest	чыканак такооч	tʃɪkanak takootʃ
back (backrest)	жөлөнгүч	dʒøløngytʃ
drawer	суурма	suurma

70. Bedding

bedclothes	шейшеп	ʃejʃep
pillow	жаздык	dʒazdɪk
pillowcase	жаздык кап	dʒazdɪk kap
duvet, comforter	жууркан	dʒuurkan
sheet	шейшеп	ʃejʃep
bedspread	жапкыч	dʒapkɪtʃ

71. Kitchen

kitchen	ашкана	aʃkana
gas	газ	gaz
gas stove (range)	газ плитасы	gaz plitasɪ
electric stove	электр плитасы	elektr plitasɪ
oven	духовка	duxovka
microwave oven	микротолкун меши	mikrotolkun meʃi

refrigerator	муздаткыч	muzdatkɪtʃ
freezer	тоңдургуч	toŋdurgutʃ
dishwasher	идиш жуучу машина	idiʃ dʒuutʃu maʃina

meat grinder	эт туурагыч	et tuuragɪtʃ
juicer	шире сыккыч	ʃire sɪkkɪtʃ
toaster	тостер	toster
mixer	миксер	mikser

coffee machine	кофе кайнаткыч	kofe kajnatkɪtʃ
coffee pot	кофе кайнатуучу идиш	kofe kajnatuutʃu idiʃ
coffee grinder	кофе майдалагыч	kofe majdalagɪtʃ

kettle	чайнек	tʃajnek
teapot	чайнек	tʃajnek
lid	капкак	kapkak

tea strainer	чыпка	ʧıpka
spoon	кашык	kaʃik
teaspoon	чай кашык	ʧaj kaʃik
soup spoon	аш кашык	aʃ kaʃik
fork	вилка	vilka
knife	бычак	bıʧak

tableware (dishes)	идиш-аяк	idiʃ-ajak
plate (dinner ~)	табак	tabak
saucer	табак	tabak

shot glass	рюмка	rumka
glass (tumbler)	ыстакан	ıstakan
cup	чөйчөк	ʧøjʧøk

sugar bowl	кум шекер салгыч	kum ʃeker salgıʧ
salt shaker	туз салгыч	tuz salgıʧ
pepper shaker	мурч салгыч	murʧ salgıʧ
butter dish	май салгыч	maj salgıʧ

stock pot (soup pot)	мискей	miskej
frying pan (skillet)	табак	tabak
ladle	чөмүч	ʧømyʧ
colander	депкир	depkir
tray (serving ~)	батыныс	batınıs

bottle	бөтөлкө	bøtølkø
jar (glass)	банка	banka
can	банка	banka

bottle opener	ачкыч	aʧkıʧ
can opener	ачкыч	aʧkıʧ
corkscrew	штопор	ʃtopor
filter	чыпка	ʧıpka
to filter (vt)	чыпкалоо	ʧıpkaloo

| trash, garbage (food waste, etc.) | таштанды | taʃtandı |
| trash can (kitchen ~) | таштанды чака | taʃtandı ʧaka |

72. Bathroom

bathroom	ванная	vannaja
water	суу	suu
faucet	чорго	ʧorgo
hot water	ысык суу	ısık suu
cold water	муздак суу	muzdak suu

| toothpaste | тиш пастасы | tiʃ pastası |
| to brush one's teeth | тиш жуу | tiʃ dʒuu |

toothbrush	тиш щёткасы	tiʃ ʃtʃotkası
to shave (vi)	кырынуу	kırınuu
shaving foam	кырынуу үчүн көбүк	kırınuu ytʃyn købyk
razor	устара	ustara

to wash (one's hands, etc.)	жуу	dʒuu
to take a bath	жуунуу	dʒuunuu
shower	душ	duʃ
to take a shower	душка түшүү	duʃka tyʃyy

bathtub	ванна	vanna
toilet (toilet bowl)	унитаз	unitaz
sink (washbasin)	раковина	rakovina

| soap | самын | samın |
| soap dish | самын салгыч | samın salgıtʃ |

sponge	губка	gubka
shampoo	шампунь	ʃampunʲ
towel	сүлгү	sylgy
bathrobe	халат	χalat

laundry (laundering)	кир жуу	kir dʒuu
washing machine	кир жуучу машина	kir dʒuutʃu maʃina
to do the laundry	кир жуу	kir dʒuu
laundry detergent	кир жуучу порошок	kir dʒuutʃu poroʃok

73. Household appliances

TV set	сыналгы	sınalgı
tape recorder	магнитофон	magnitofon
VCR (video recorder)	видеомагнитофон	videomagnitofon
radio	үналгы	ynalgı
player (CD, MP3, etc.)	плеер	pleer

video projector	видеопроектор	videoproektor
home movie theater	үй кинотеатры	yj kinoteatrı
DVD player	DVD ойноткуч	dividi ojnotkutʃ
amplifier	күчөткүч	kytʃøtkytʃ
video game console	оюн приставкасы	ojun pristavkası

video camera	видеокамера	videokamera
camera (photo)	фотоаппарат	fotoapparat
digital camera	санарип камерасы	sanarip kamerası

vacuum cleaner	чаң соргуч	tʃaŋ sorgutʃ
iron (e.g., steam ~)	үтүк	ytyk
ironing board	үтүктөөчү тактай	ytyktøøtʃy taktaj
telephone	телефон	telefon
cell phone	мобилдик	mobildik

| typewriter | машинка | maʃinka |
| sewing machine | кийим тигүүчү машинка | kijim tigyytʃy maʃinka |

microphone	микрофон	mikrofon
headphones	кулакчын	kulaktʃın
remote control (TV)	пульт	pulʲt

CD, compact disc	CD, компакт-диск	sidi, kompakt-disk
cassette, tape	кассета	kasseta
vinyl record	пластинка	plastinka

T&P BOOKS

THE EARTH. WEATHER

T&P Books Publishing

74. Outer space

space	космос	kosmos
space (as adj)	космос	kosmos
outer space	космос мейкиндиги	kosmos mejkindigi
world	дүйнө	dyjnø
universe	аалам	aalam
galaxy	галактика	galaktika
star	жылдыз	dʒıldız
constellation	жылдыздар	dʒıldızdar
planet	планета	planeta
satellite	жолдош	dʒoldoʃ
meteorite	метеорит	meteorit
comet	комета	kometa
asteroid	астероид	asteroid
orbit	орбита	orbita
to revolve	айлануу	ajlanuu
(~ around the Earth)		
atmosphere	атмосфера	atmosfera
the Sun	күн	kyn
solar system	күн системасы	kyn sisteması
solar eclipse	күндүн тутулушу	kyndyn tutuluʃu
the Earth	Жер	dʒer
the Moon	Ай	aj
Mars	Марс	mars
Venus	Венера	venera
Jupiter	Юпитер	jupiter
Saturn	Сатурн	saturn
Mercury	Меркурий	merkurij
Uranus	Уран	uran
Neptune	Нептун	neptun
Pluto	Плутон	pluton
Milky Way	Саманчынын жолу	samantʃının dʒolu
Great Bear (Ursa Major)	Чоң Жетиген	tʃoŋ dʒetigen
North Star	Полярдык Жылдыз	polʲardık dʒıldız
Martian	марсианин	marsianin
extraterrestrial (n)	инопланетянин	inoplanetʲanin

| alien | келгин | kelgin |
| flying saucer | учуучу табак | utʃuutʃu tabak |

spaceship	космос кемеси	kosmos kemesi
space station	орбитадагы станция	orbitadagı stantsija
blast-off	старт	start

engine	кыймылдаткыч	kıjmıldatkıtʃ
nozzle	сопло	soplo
fuel	күйүүчү май	kyjyytʃy may

cockpit, flight deck	кабина	kabina
antenna	антенна	antenna
porthole	иллюминатор	illʉminator
solar panel	күн батареясы	kyn batarejası
spacesuit	скафандр	skafandr

| weightlessness | салмаксыздык | salmaksızdık |
| oxygen | кислород | kislorod |

| docking (in space) | жалгаштыруу | dʒalgaʃtıruu |
| to dock (vi, vt) | жалгаштыруу | dʒalgaʃtıruu |

observatory	обсерватория	observatorija
telescope	телескоп	teleskop
to observe (vt)	байкоо	bajkoo
to explore (vt)	изилдөө	izildøø

75. The Earth

the Earth	Жер	dʒer
the globe (the Earth)	жер шары	dʒer ʃarı
planet	планета	planeta

atmosphere	атмосфера	atmosfera
geography	география	geografija
nature	табийгат	tabijgat

globe (table ~)	глобус	globus
map	карта	karta
atlas	атлас	atlas

Europe	Европа	evropa
Asia	Азия	azija
Africa	Африка	afrika
Australia	Австралия	avstralija

America	Америка	amerika
North America	Северная Америка	severnaja amerika
South America	Южная Америка	jʉdʒnaja amerika

Antarctica	Антарктида	antarktida
the Arctic	Арктика	arktika

76. Cardinal directions

north	түндүк	tyndyk
to the north	түндүккө	tyndykkø
in the north	түндүктө	tyndyktø
northern (adj)	түндүк	tyndyk

south	түштүк	tyʃtyk
to the south	түштүккө	tyʃtykkø
in the south	түштүктө	tyʃtyktø
southern (adj)	түштүк	tyʃtyk

west	батыш	batıʃ
to the west	батышка	batıʃka
in the west	батышта	batıʃta
western (adj)	батыш	batıʃ

east	чыгыш	tʃıgıʃ
to the east	чыгышка	tʃıgıʃka
in the east	чыгышта	tʃıgıʃta
eastern (adj)	чыгыш	tʃıgıʃ

77. Sea. Ocean

sea	деңиз	deŋiz
ocean	мухит	muχit
gulf (bay)	булуң	buluŋ
straits	кысык	kısık

land (solid ground)	жер	dʒer
continent (mainland)	материк	materik

island	арал	aral
peninsula	жарым арал	dʒarım aral
archipelago	архипелаг	arχipelag

bay, cove	булуң	buluŋ
harbor	гавань	gavanʲ
lagoon	лагуна	laguna
cape	тумшук	tumʃuk

atoll	атолл	atoll
reef	риф	rif
coral	маржан	mardʒan
coral reef	маржан рифи	mardʒan rifi

deep (adj)	терең	tereŋ
depth (deep water)	терендик	tereŋdik
abyss	түбү жок	tyby dʒok
trench (e.g., Mariana ~)	ойдуң	ojduŋ

| current (Ocean ~) | агым | agım |
| to surround (bathe) | курчап туруу | kurtʃap turuu |

| shore | жээк | dʒeek |
| coast | жээк | dʒeek |

flow (flood tide)	суунун көтөрүлүшү	suunun køtørylyʃy
ebb (ebb tide)	суунун тартылуусу	suunun tartıluusu
shoal	тайыздык	tajızdık
bottom (~ of the sea)	суунун түбү	suunun tyby

wave	толкун	tolkun
crest (~ of a wave)	толкундун кыры	tolkundun kırı
spume (sea foam)	көбүк	købyk

storm (sea storm)	бороон чапкын	boroon tʃapkın
hurricane	бороон	boroon
tsunami	цунами	tsunami
calm (dead ~)	штиль	ʃtilʲ
quiet, calm (adj)	тынч	tıntʃ

| pole | уюл | ujʉl |
| polar (adj) | полярдык | polʲardık |

latitude	кеңдик	keŋdik
longitude	узундук	uzunduk
parallel	параллель	parallelʲ
equator	экватор	ekvator

sky	асман	asman
horizon	горизонт	gorizont
air	аба	aba

lighthouse	маяк	majak
to dive (vi)	сүңгүү	syŋgyy
to sink (ab. boat)	чөгүп кетүү	tʃøgyp ketyy
treasures	казына	kazına

78. Seas' and Oceans' names

Atlantic Ocean	Атлантика мухити	atlantika muχiti
Indian Ocean	Индия мухити	indija muχiti
Pacific Ocean	Тынч мухити	tıntʃ muχiti
Arctic Ocean	Түндүк Муз мухити	tyndyk muz muχiti
Black Sea	Кара деңиз	kara deŋiz

Red Sea	Кызыл деңиз	kızıl deŋiz
Yellow Sea	Сары деңиз	sarı deŋiz
White Sea	Ак деңиз	ak deŋiz

Caspian Sea	Каспий деңизи	kaspij deŋizi
Dead Sea	Өлүк деңиз	ølyk deŋiz
Mediterranean Sea	Жер Ортолук деңиз	dʒer ortoluk deŋiz

| Aegean Sea | Эгей деңизи | egej deŋizi |
| Adriatic Sea | Адриатика деңизи | adriatika deŋizi |

Arabian Sea	Аравия деңизи	aravija deŋizi
Sea of Japan	Япон деңизи	japon deŋizi
Bering Sea	Беринг деңизи	bering deŋizi
South China Sea	Түштүк-Кытай деңизи	tyʃtyk-kıtaj deŋizi

Coral Sea	Маржан деңизи	mardʒan deŋizi
Tasman Sea	Тасман деңизи	tasman deŋizi
Caribbean Sea	Кариб деңизи	karib deŋizi

| Barents Sea | Баренц деңизи | barents deŋizi |
| Kara Sea | Карск деңизи | karsk deŋizi |

North Sea	Түндүк деңиз	tyndyk deŋiz
Baltic Sea	Балтика деңизи	baltika deŋizi
Norwegian Sea	Норвегиялык деңизи	norvegijalık deŋizi

79. Mountains

mountain	тоо	too
mountain range	тоо тизмеги	too tizmegi
mountain ridge	тоо кыркалары	too kırkaları

summit, top	чоку	tʃoku
peak	чоку	tʃoku
foot (~ of the mountain)	тоо этеги	too etegi
slope (mountainside)	эңкейиш	eŋkejiʃ

volcano	вулкан	vulkan
active volcano	күйүп жаткан	kyjyp dʒatkan
dormant volcano	өчүп калган вулкан	øtʃyp kalgan vulkan

eruption	атырылып чыгуу	atırılıp tʃıguu
crater	кратер	krater
magma	магма	magma
lava	лава	lava
molten (~ lava)	кызыган	kızıgan

| canyon | каньон | kanʲon |
| gorge | капчыгай | kaptʃıgaj |

| crevice | жарака | dʒaraka |
| abyss (chasm) | жар | dʒar |

pass, col	ашуу	aʃuu
plateau	дөңсөө	døŋsøø
cliff	зоока	zooka
hill	дөбө	døbø

glacier	муз	muz
waterfall	шаркыратма	ʃarkıratma
geyser	гейзер	gejzer
lake	көл	køl

plain	түздүк	tyzdyk
landscape	теребел	terebel
echo	жаңырык	dʒaŋırık

alpinist	альпинист	alʲpinist
rock climber	скалолаз	skalolaz
to conquer (in climbing)	багындыруу	bagındıruu
climb (an easy ~)	тоонун чокусуна чыгуу	toonun tʃokusuna tʃıguu

80. Mountains names

The Alps	Альп тоолору	alʲp tooloru
Mont Blanc	Монблан	monblan
The Pyrenees	Пиреней тоолору	pirenej tooloru

The Carpathians	Карпат тоолору	karpat tooloru
The Ural Mountains	Урал тоолору	ural tooloru
The Caucasus Mountains	Кавказ тоолору	kavkaz tooloru
Mount Elbrus	Эльбрус	elʲbrus

The Altai Mountains	Алтai тоолору	altaj tooloru
The Tian Shan	Тянь-Шань	tjanʲ-ʃanʲ
The Pamir Mountains	Памир тоолору	pamir tooloru
The Himalayas	Гималай тоолору	gimalaj tooloru
Mount Everest	Эверест	everest

| The Andes | Анд тоолору | and tooloru |
| Mount Kilimanjaro | Килиманджаро | kilimandʒaro |

81. Rivers

river	дарыя	darıja
spring (natural source)	булак	bulak
riverbed (river channel)	сай	saj
basin (river valley)	бассейн	bassejn

to flow into ...	... куюу	... kujʉu
tributary	куйма	kujma
bank (of river)	жээк	ʤeek

current (stream)	агым	agım
downstream (adv)	агым боюнча	agım bojʉnʧa
upstream (adv)	агымга каршы	agımga karʃı

inundation	ташкын	taʃkın
flooding	суу ташкыны	suu taʃkını
to overflow (vi)	дайранын ташышы	dajranın taʃıʃı
to flood (vt)	суу каптоо	suu kaptoo

| shallow (shoal) | тайыздык | tajızdık |
| rapids | босого | bosogo |

dam	тогоон	togoon
canal	канал	kanal
reservoir (artificial lake)	суу сактагыч	suu saktagıʧ
sluice, lock	шлюз	ʃlʉz

water body (pond, etc.)	көлмө	kølmø
swamp (marshland)	саз	saz
bog, marsh	баткак	batkak
whirlpool	айлампа	ajlampa

stream (brook)	суу	suu
drinking (ab. water)	ичилчү суу	iʧilʧy suu
fresh (~ water)	тузсуз	tuzsuz

| ice | муз | muz |
| to freeze over (ab. river, etc.) | тоңуп калуу | toŋup kaluu |

82. Rivers' names

| Seine | Сена | sena |
| Loire | Луара | luara |

Thames	Темза	temza
Rhine	Рейн	rejn
Danube	Дунай	dunaj

Volga	Волга	volga
Don	Дон	don
Lena	Лена	lena

Yellow River	Хуанхэ	χuanχe
Yangtze	Янцзы	janʦzı
Mekong	Меконг	mekong

Ganges	Ганг	gang
Nile River	Нил	nil
Congo River	Конго	kongo
Okavango River	Окаванго	okavango
Zambezi River	Замбези	zambezi
Limpopo River	Лимпопо	limpopo
Mississippi River	Миссисипи	missisipi

83. Forest

| forest, wood | токой | tokoj |
| forest (as adj) | токойлуу | tokojluu |

thick forest	чытырман токой	tʃıtırman tokoj
grove	токойчо	tokojtʃo
forest clearing	аянт	ajant

| thicket | бадал | badal |
| scrubland | бадал | badal |

| footpath (troddenpath) | чыйыр жол | tʃıjır dʒol |
| gully | жар | dʒar |

tree	дарак	darak
leaf	жалбырак	dʒalbırak
leaves (foliage)	жалбырак	dʒalbırak

fall of leaves	жалбырак түшүү мезгили	dʒalbırak tyʃyy mezgili
to fall (ab. leaves)	түшүү	tyʃyy
top (of the tree)	чоку	tʃoku

branch	бутак	butak
bough	бутак	butak
bud (on shrub, tree)	бүчүр	bytʃyr
needle (of pine tree)	ийне	ijne
pine cone	тобурчак	toburtʃak

tree hollow	көңдөй	køŋdøj
nest	уя	uja
burrow (animal hole)	ийин	ijin

trunk	сеңгек	søŋgøk
root	тамыр	tamır
bark	кыртыш	kırtıʃ
moss	мох	moχ

| to uproot (remove trees or tree stumps) | дүмүрүн казуу | dymyryn kazuu |
| to chop down | кыюу | kıjuu |

| to deforest (vt) | токойду кыюу | tokojdu kıjʉu |
| tree stump | дүмүр | dymyr |

campfire	от	ot
forest fire	өрт	ørt
to extinguish (vt)	өчүрүү	øʧyryy

forest ranger	токойчу	tokojʧu
protection	өсүмдүктөрдү коргоо	øsymdyktørdy korgoo
to protect (~ nature)	сактоо	saktoo
poacher	браконьер	brakonjer
steel trap	капкан	kapkan

to pick (mushrooms)	терүү	teryy
to pick (berries)	терүү	teryy
to lose one's way	адашып кетүү	adaʃıp ketyy

84. Natural resources

natural resources	жаратылыш байлыктары	ʤaratılıʃ bajlıktarı
minerals	пайдалуу кендер	pajdaluu kender
deposits	кен	ken
field (e.g., oilfield)	кендүү жер	kendyy ʤer

to mine (extract)	казуу	kazuu
mining (extraction)	казуу	kazuu
ore	кен	ken
mine (e.g., for coal)	шахта	ʃaxta
shaft (mine ~)	шахта	ʃaxta
miner	кенчи	kenʧi

| gas (natural ~) | газ | gaz |
| gas pipeline | газопровод | gazoprovod |

oil (petroleum)	мунайзат	munajzat
oil pipeline	мунайзар түтүгү	munajzar tytygy
oil well	мунайзат скважинасы	munajzat skvadʒinası
derrick (tower)	мунайзат мунарасы	munajzat munarası
tanker	танкер	tanker

sand	кум	kum
limestone	акиташ	akitaʃ
gravel	шагыл	ʃagıl
peat	торф	torf
clay	ылай	ılaj
coal	көмүр	kømyr

| iron (ore) | темир | temir |
| gold | алтын | altın |

silver	күмүш	kymyʃ
nickel	никель	nikelʲ
copper	жез	dʒez

zinc	цинк	tsɪnk
manganese	марганец	marganets
mercury	сымап	sɪmap
lead	коргошун	korgoʃun

mineral	минерал	mineral
crystal	кристалл	kristall
marble	мрамор	mramor
uranium	уран	uran

85. Weather

weather	аба-ырайы	aba-ɪrajɪ
weather forecast	аба-ырайы боюнча маалымат	aba-ɪrajɪ bojʉntʃa maalɪmat
temperature	температура	temperatura
thermometer	термометр	termometr
barometer	барометр	barometr

| humid (adj) | нымдуу | nɪmduu |
| humidity | ным | nɪm |

heat (extreme ~)	ысык	ɪsɪk
hot (torrid)	кыйын ысык	kɪjɪn ɪsɪk
it's hot	ысык	ɪsɪk

| it's warm | жылуу | dʒɪluu |
| warm (moderately hot) | жылуу | dʒɪluu |

| it's cold | суук | suuk |
| cold (adj) | суук | suuk |

sun	күн	kyn
to shine (vi)	күн тийүү	kyn tijyy
sunny (day)	күн ачык	kyn atʃik
to come up (vi)	чыгуу	tʃɪguu
to set (vi)	батуу	batuu

cloud	булут	bulut
cloudy (adj)	булуттуу	buluttuu
rain cloud	булут	bulut
somber (gloomy)	күн бүркөк	kyn byrkøk

rain	жамгыр	dʒamgɪr
it's raining	жамгыр жаап жатат	dʒamgɪr dʒaap dʒatat
rainy (~ day, weather)	жаандуу	dʒaanduu

to drizzle (vi)	дыбыратуу	dıbıratuu
pouring rain	нөшөрлөгөн жаан	nøʃørløgøn dʒaan
downpour	нөшөр	nøʃør
heavy (e.g., ~ rain)	катуу	katuu
puddle	көлчүк	køltʃyk
to get wet (in rain)	суу болуу	suu boluu

fog (mist)	туман	tuman
foggy	тумандуу	tumanduu
snow	кар	kar
it's snowing	кар жаап жатат	kar dʒaap dʒatat

86. Severe weather. Natural disasters

thunderstorm	чагылгандуу жаан	tʃagılganduu dʒaan
lightning (~ strike)	чагылган	tʃagılgan
to flash (vi)	жарк этүү	dʒark etyy

thunder	күн күркүрөө	kyn kyrkyrøø
to thunder (vi)	күн күркүрөө	kyn kyrkyrøø
it's thundering	күн күркүрөп жатат	kyn kyrkyrøp dʒatat

| hail | мөндүр | møndyr |
| it's hailing | мөндүр түшүп жатат | møndyr tyʃyp dʒatat |

| to flood (vt) | суу каптоо | suu kaptoo |
| flood, inundation | ташкын | taʃkın |

earthquake	жер титирөө	dʒer titirøø
tremor, shoke	жердин силкиниши	dʒerdin silkiniʃi
epicenter	эпицентр	epitsentr

| eruption | атырылып чыгуу | atırılıp tʃıguu |
| lava | лава | lava |

twister	куюн	kujʉn
tornado	торнадо	tornado
typhoon	тайфун	tajfun

hurricane	бороон	boroon
storm	бороон чапкын	boroon tʃapkın
tsunami	цунами	tsunami

cyclone	циклон	tsıklon
bad weather	жаан-чачындуу күн	dʒaan-tʃatʃınduu kyn
fire (accident)	өрт	ørt
disaster	кыйроо	kıjroo
meteorite	метеорит	meteorit
avalanche	көчкү	køtʃky
snowslide	кар көчкүсү	kar køtʃkysy

blizzard	**кар бороону**	kar boroonu
snowstorm	**бурганак**	burganak

FAUNA

T&P Books Publishing

87. Mammals. Predators

predator	жырткыч	dʒɪrtkɪtʃ
tiger	жолборс	dʒolbors
lion	арстан	arstan
wolf	карышкыр	karɪʃkɪr
fox	түлкү	tylky
jaguar	ягуар	jaguar
leopard	леопард	leopard
cheetah	гепард	gepard
black panther	пантера	pantera
puma	пума	puma
snow leopard	илбирс	ilbirs
lynx	сүлөөсүн	syløøsyn
coyote	койот	kojot
jackal	чөө	tʃøø
hyena	гиена	giena

88. Wild animals

animal	жаныбар	dʒanɪbar
beast (animal)	жапайы жаныбар	dʒapajɪ dʒanɪbar
squirrel	тыйын чычкан	tɪjɪn tʃɪtʃkan
hedgehog	кирпичечен	kirpitʃetʃen
hare	коен	koen
rabbit	коен	koen
badger	кашкулак	kaʃkulak
raccoon	енот	enot
hamster	хомяк	χomʲak
marmot	суур	suur
mole	момолой	momoloj
mouse	чычкан	tʃɪtʃkan
rat	келемиш	kelemiʃ
bat	жарганат	dʒarganat
ermine	арс чычкан	ars tʃɪtʃkan
sable	киш	kiʃ
marten	суусар	suusar

| weasel | ласка | laska |
| mink | норка | norka |

| beaver | кемчет | kemʧet |
| otter | кундуз | kunduz |

horse	жылкы	dʒɯlkɯ
moose	багыш	bagɯʃ
deer	бугу	bugu
camel	төө	tøø

bison	бизон	bizon
wisent	зубр	zubr
buffalo	буйвол	bujvol

zebra	зебра	zebra
antelope	антилопа	antilopa
roe deer	элик	elik
fallow deer	лань	lanʲ
chamois	жейрен	dʒejren
wild boar	каман	kaman

whale	кит	kit
seal	тюлень	tʉlenʲ
walrus	морж	mordʒ
fur seal	деңиз мышыгы	deŋiz mɯʃɯgɯ
dolphin	дельфин	delʲfin

bear	аюу	ajʉu
polar bear	ак аюу	ak ajʉu
panda	панда	panda

monkey	маймыл	majmɯl
chimpanzee	шимпанзе	ʃimpanze
orangutan	орангутанг	orangutang
gorilla	горилла	gorilla
macaque	макака	makaka
gibbon	гиббон	gibbon

| elephant | пил | pil |
| rhinoceros | керик | kerik |

| giraffe | жираф | dʒiraf |
| hippopotamus | бегемот | begemot |

| kangaroo | кенгуру | kenguru |
| koala (bear) | коала | koala |

mongoose	мангуст	mangust
chinchilla	шиншилла	ʃinʃilla
skunk	скунс	skuns
porcupine	чүткөр	ʧytkør

89. Domestic animals

cat	ургаачы мышык	urgaatʃı mıʃık
tomcat	эркек мышык	erkek mıʃık
dog	ит	it

horse	жылкы	dʒılkı
stallion (male horse)	айгыр	ajgır
mare	бээ	bee

cow	уй	uj
bull	бука	buka
ox	өгүз	øgyz

sheep (ewe)	кой	koj
ram	кочкор	kotʃkor
goat	эчки	etʃki
billy goat, he-goat	теке	teke

| donkey | эшек | eʃek |
| mule | качыр | katʃır |

pig, hog	чочко	tʃotʃko
piglet	торопой	toropoj
rabbit	коен	koen

| hen (chicken) | тоок | took |
| rooster | короз | koroz |

duck	өрдөк	ørdøk
drake	эркек өрдөк	erkek ørdøk
goose	каз	kaz

| tom turkey, gobbler | күрп | kyrp |
| turkey (hen) | ургаачы күрп | urgaatʃı kyrp |

domestic animals	үй жаныбарлары	yj dʒanıbarları
tame (e.g., ~ hamster)	колго үйрөтүлгөн	kolgo yjrøtylgøn
to tame (vt)	колго үйрөтүү	kolgo yjrøtyy
to breed (vt)	өстүрүү	østyryy

farm	ферма	ferma
poultry	үй канаттулары	yj kanattuları
cattle	мал	mal
herd (cattle)	бада	bada

stable	аткана	atkana
pigpen	чочкокана	tʃotʃkokana
cowshed	уйкана	ujkana
rabbit hutch	коенкана	koenkana
hen house	тоокана	tookana

90. Birds

bird	куш	kuʃ
pigeon	көгүчкөн	køgytʃkøn
sparrow	таранчы	tarantʃı
tit (great tit)	синица	sinitsa
magpie	сагызган	sagızgan

raven	кузгун	kuzgun
crow	карга	karga
jackdaw	таан	taan
rook	чаркарга	tʃarkarga

duck	өрдөк	ørdøk
goose	каз	kaz
pheasant	кыргоол	kırgool

eagle	бүркүт	byrkyt
hawk	ителги	itelgi
falcon	шумкар	ʃumkar
vulture	жору	dʒoru
condor (Andean ~)	кондор	kondor

swan	аккуу	akkuu
crane	турна	turna
stork	илегилек	ilegilek

parrot	тотукуш	totukuʃ
hummingbird	колибри	kolibri
peacock	тоос	toos

ostrich	төө куш	tøø kuʃ
heron	көк кытан	køk kıtan
flamingo	фламинго	flamingo
pelican	биргазан	birgazan

| nightingale | булбул | bulbul |
| swallow | чабалекей | tʃabalekej |

thrush	таркылдак	tarkıldak
song thrush	сайрагыч таркылдак	sajragıtʃ tarkıldak
blackbird	кара таңдай таркылдак	kara taŋdaj tarkıldak

swift	кардыгач	kardıgatʃ
lark	торгой	torgoj
quail	бөдөнө	bødønø

woodpecker	тоңкулдак	toŋkuldak
cuckoo	күкүк	kykyk
owl	мыкый үкү	mıkıj yky
eagle owl	үкү	yky

wood grouse	керең кур	kereŋ kur
black grouse	кара кур	kara kur
partridge	кекилик	kekilik

starling	чыйырчык	ʧijirʧık
canary	канарейка	kanarejka
hazel grouse	токой чили	tokoj ʧili
chaffinch	зяблик	zʲablik
bullfinch	снегирь	snegirʲ

seagull	ак чардак	ak ʧardak
albatross	альбатрос	alʲbatros
penguin	пингвин	pingvin

91. Fish. Marine animals

bream	лещ	leʃʧ
carp	карп	karp
perch	окунь	okunʲ
catfish	жаян	dʒajan
pike	чортон	ʧorton

| salmon | лосось | lososʲ |
| sturgeon | осётр | osʲotr |

herring	сельдь	selʲdʲ
Atlantic salmon	сёмга	sʲomga
mackerel	скумбрия	skumbrija
flatfish	камбала	kambala

zander, pike perch	судак	sudak
cod	треска	treska
tuna	тунец	tunets
trout	форель	forelʲ

eel	угорь	ugorʲ
electric ray	скат	skat
moray eel	мурена	murena
piranha	пиранья	piranja

shark	акула	akula
dolphin	дельфин	delʲfin
whale	кит	kit

crab	краб	krab
jellyfish	медуза	meduza
octopus	сегиз бут	segiz but

| starfish | деңиз жылдызы | deŋiz dʒıldızı |
| sea urchin | деңиз кирписи | deŋiz kirpisi |

seahorse	деңиз тайы	deŋiz tajı
oyster	устрица	ustritsa
shrimp	креветка	krevetka
lobster	омар	omar
spiny lobster	лангуст	langust

92. Amphibians. Reptiles

| snake | жылан | dʒılan |
| venomous (snake) | уулуу | uuluu |

viper	кара чаар жылан	kara tʃaar dʒılan
cobra	кобра	kobra
python	питон	piton
boa	удав	udav

grass snake	сары жылан	sarı dʒılan
rattle snake	шакылдак жылан	ʃakıldak dʒılan
anaconda	анаконда	anakonda

lizard	кескелдирик	keskeldirik
iguana	игуана	iguana
monitor lizard	эчкемер	etʃkemer
salamander	саламандра	salamandra
chameleon	хамелеон	χameleon
scorpion	чаян	tʃajan

turtle	ташбака	taʃbaka
frog	бака	baka
toad	курбака	kurbaka
crocodile	крокодил	krokodil

93. Insects

insect, bug	курт-кумурска	kurt-kumurska
butterfly	көпөлөк	køpøløk
ant	кумурска	kumurska
fly	чымын	tʃımın
mosquito	чиркей	tʃirkej
beetle	коңуз	koŋuz

wasp	аары	aarı
bee	бал аары	bal aarı
bumblebee	жапан аары	dʒapan aarı
gadfly (botfly)	көгөөн	køgøøn

| spider | жөргөмүш | dʒørgømyʃ |
| spiderweb | желе | dʒele |

dragonfly	**ийнелик**	ijnelik
grasshopper	**чегиртке**	ʧegirtke
moth (night butterfly)	**көпөлөк**	køpøløk
cockroach	**таракан**	tarakan
tick	**кене**	kene
flea	**бүргө**	byrgø
midge	**майда чымын**	majda ʧımın
locust	**чегиртке**	ʧegirtke
snail	**үлүл**	ylyl
cricket	**кара чегиртке**	kara ʧegirtke
lightning bug	**жалтырак коңуз**	ʤaltırak koŋuz
ladybug	**айланкөчөк**	ajlankøʧøk
cockchafer	**саратан коңуз**	saratan koŋuz
leech	**сүлүк**	sylyk
caterpillar	**каз таман**	kaz taman
earthworm	**жер курту**	ʤer kurtu
larva	**курт**	kurt

T&P BOOKS

FLORA

T&P Books Publishing

tree	дарак	darak
deciduous (adj)	жалбырактуу	dʒalbıraktuu
coniferous (adj)	ийне жалбырактуулар	ijne dʒalbıraktuular
evergreen (adj)	дайым жашыл	dajım dʒaʃıl

apple tree	алма бак	alma bak
pear tree	алмурут бак	almurut bak
sweet cherry tree	гилас	gilas
sour cherry tree	алча	altʃa
plum tree	кара өрүк	kara øryk

birch	ак кайың	ak kajıŋ
oak	эмен	emen
linden tree	жөкө дарак	dʒøkø darak
aspen	бай терек	baj terek
maple	клён	klʲon

spruce	кара карагай	kara karagaj
pine	карагай	karagaj
larch	лиственница	listvennitsa

| fir tree | пихта | piχta |
| cedar | кедр | kedr |

| poplar | терек | terek |
| rowan | четин | tʃetin |

| willow | мажүрүм тал | madʒyrym tal |
| alder | ольха | olʲχa |

| beech | бук | buk |
| elm | кара жыгач | kara dʒıgatʃ |

| ash (tree) | ясень | jasenʲ |
| chestnut | каштан | kaʃtan |

magnolia	магнолия	magnolija
palm tree	пальма	palʲma
cypress	кипарис	kiparis

mangrove	мангро дарагы	mangro daragı
baobab	баобаб	baobab
eucalyptus	эвкалипт	evkalipt
sequoia	секвойя	sekvoja

95. Shrubs

bush	бадал	badal
shrub	бадал	badal
grapevine	жүзүм	dʒyzym
vineyard	жүзүмдүк	dʒyzymdyk
raspberry bush	дан куурай	dan kuuraj
blackcurrant bush	кара карагат	kara karagat
redcurrant bush	кызыл карагат	kızıl karagat
gooseberry bush	крыжовник	krıdʒovnik
acacia	акация	akaʦija
barberry	бөрү карагат	børy karagat
jasmine	жасмин	dʒasmin
juniper	кара арча	kara artʃa
rosebush	роза бадалы	roza badalı
dog rose	ит мурун	it murun

96. Fruits. Berries

fruit	мөмө-жемиш	mømø-dʒemiʃ
fruits	мөмө-жемиш	mømø-dʒemiʃ
apple	алма	alma
pear	алмурут	almurut
plum	кара өрүк	kara øryk
strawberry (garden ~)	кулпунай	kulpunaj
sour cherry	алча	altʃa
sweet cherry	гилас	gilas
grape	жүзүм	dʒyzym
raspberry	дан куурай	dan kuuraj
blackcurrant	кара карагат	kara karagat
redcurrant	кызыл карагат	kızıl karagat
gooseberry	крыжовник	krıdʒovnik
cranberry	клюква	klʉkva
orange	апельсин	apelʲsin
mandarin	мандарин	mandarin
pineapple	ананас	ananas
banana	банан	banan
date	курма	kurma
lemon	лимон	limon
apricot	өрүк	øryk

peach	шабдаалы	ʃabdaalı
kiwi	киви	kivi
grapefruit	грейпфрут	grejpfrut

berry	жер жемиш	dʒer dʒemiʃ
berries	жер жемиштер	dʒer dʒemiʃter
cowberry	брусника	brusnika
wild strawberry	кызылгат	kızılgat
bilberry	кара моюл	kara mojʉl

97. Flowers. Plants

| flower | гүл | gyl |
| bouquet (of flowers) | десте | deste |

rose (flower)	роза	roza
tulip	жоогазын	dʒoogazın
carnation	гвоздика	gvozdika
gladiolus	гладиолус	gladiolus

cornflower	ботокөз	botokøz
harebell	коңгуроо гүл	koŋguroo gyl
dandelion	каакым-кукум	kaakım-kukum
camomile	ромашка	romaʃka

aloe	алоэ	aloe
cactus	кактус	kaktus
rubber plant, ficus	фикус	fikus

lily	лилия	lilija
geranium	герань	geranʲ
hyacinth	гиацинт	giatsint

mimosa	мимоза	mimoza
narcissus	нарцисс	nartsiss
nasturtium	настурция	nasturtsija

orchid	орхидея	orχideja
peony	пион	pion
violet	бинапша	binapʃa

pansy	алагүл	alagyl
forget-me-not	незабудка	nezabudka
daisy	маргаритка	margaritka

poppy	кызгалдак	kızgaldak
hemp	наша	naʃa
mint	жалбыз	dʒalbız
lily of the valley	ландыш	landıʃ
snowdrop	байчечекей	bajtʃetʃekej

nettle	чалкан	tʃalkan
sorrel	ат кулак	at kulak
water lily	чөмүч баш	tʃømytʃ baʃ
fern	папоротник	paporotnik
lichen	лишайник	liʃajnik

conservatory (greenhouse)	күнөскана	kynøskana
lawn	газон	gazon
flowerbed	клумба	klumba

plant	өсүмдүк	øsymdyk
grass	чөп	tʃøp
blade of grass	бир тал чөп	bir tal tʃøp

leaf	жалбырак	dʒalbırak
petal	гүлдүн желекчеси	gyldyn dʒelektʃesi
stem	сабак	sabak
tuber	жемиш тамыр	dʒemiʃ tamır

| young plant (shoot) | өсмө | øsmø |
| thorn | тикен | tiken |

to blossom (vi)	гүлдөө	gyldøø
to fade, to wither	соолуу	sooluu
smell (odor)	жыт	dʒıt
to cut (flowers)	кесүү	kesyy
to pick (a flower)	үзүү	yzyy

98. Cereals, grains

grain	дан	dan
cereal crops	дан эгиндери	dan eginderi
ear (of barley, etc.)	машак	maʃak

wheat	буудай	buudaj
rye	кара буудай	kara buudaj
oats	сулу	sulu

| millet | таруу | taruu |
| barley | арпа | arpa |

corn	жүгөрү	dʒygøry
rice	күрүч	kyrytʃ
buckwheat	гречиха	gretʃixa

pea plant	нокот	nokot
kidney bean	төө буурчак	tøø buurtʃak
soy	соя	soja
lentil	жасмык	dʒasmık
beans (pulse crops)	буурчак	buurtʃak

COUNTRIES OF
THE WORLD

T&P Books Publishing

Afghanistan	Ооганстан	ooganstan
Albania	Албания	albanija
Argentina	Аргентина	argentina
Armenia	Армения	armenija
Australia	Австралия	avstralija
Austria	Австрия	avstrija
Azerbaijan	Азербайжан	azerbajdʒan

The Bahamas	Багам аралдары	bagam araldarı
Bangladesh	Бангладеш	bangladeʃ
Belarus	Беларусь	belarusʲ
Belgium	Бельгия	belʲgija
Bolivia	Боливия	bolivija
Bosnia and Herzegovina	Босния жана	bosnija dʒana
Brazil	Бразилия	brazilija
Bulgaria	Болгария	bolgarija
Cambodia	Камбожа	kambodʒa
Canada	Канада	kanada
Chile	Чили	tʃili
China	Кытай	kıtaj
Colombia	Колумбия	kolumbija
Croatia	Хорватия	χorvatija
Cuba	Куба	kuba
Cyprus	Кипр	kipr
Czech Republic	Чехия	tʃeχija

| Denmark | Дания | danija |
| Dominican Republic | Доминикан Республикасы | dominikan respublikası |

Ecuador	Эквадор	ekvador
Egypt	Египет	egipet
England	Англия	anglija
Estonia	Эстония	estonija
Finland	Финляндия	finlʲandija
France	Франция	frantsija
French Polynesia	Француз Полинезиясы	frantsuz polinezijası

Georgia	Грузия	gruzija
Germany	Германия	germanija
Ghana	Гана	gana
Great Britain	Улуу Британия	uluu britanija
Greece	Греция	gretsija
Haiti	Гаити	gaiti
Hungary	Венгрия	vengrija

100. Countries. Part 2

Iceland	Исландия	islandija
India	Индия	indija
Indonesia	Индонезия	indonezija
Iran	Иран	iran
Iraq	Ирак	irak
Ireland	Ирландия	irlandija
Israel	Израиль	izrailʲ
Italy	Италия	italija

Jamaica	Ямайка	jamajka
Japan	Япония	japonija
Jordan	Иордания	iordanija
Kazakhstan	Казакстан	kazakstan
Kenya	Кения	kenija
Kirghizia	Кыргызстан	kırgızstan
Kuwait	Кувейт	kuvejt
Laos	Лаос	laos
Latvia	Латвия	latvija
Lebanon	Ливан	livan
Libya	Ливия	livija
Liechtenstein	Лихтенштейн	liχtenʃtejn
Lithuania	Литва	litva
Luxembourg	Люксембург	lɵksemburg
Macedonia (Republic of ~)	Македония	makedonija
Madagascar	Мадагаскар	madagaskar
Malaysia	Малазия	malazija
Malta	Мальта	malʲta
Mexico	Мексика	meksika
Moldova, Moldavia	Молдова	moldova

Monaco	Монако	monako
Mongolia	Монголия	mongolija
Montenegro	Черногория	tʃernogorija
Morocco	Марокко	marokko
Myanmar	Мьянма	mjanma

Namibia	Намибия	namibija
Nepal	Непал	nepal
Netherlands	Нидерланддар	niderlanddar
New Zealand	Жаңы Зеландия	dʒaŋı zelandija
North Korea	Түндүк Корея	tundyk koreja
Norway	Норвегия	norvegija

101. Countries. Part 3

Pakistan	Пакистан	pakistan
Palestine	Палестина	palestina

Panama	Панама	panama
Paraguay	Парагвай	paragvaj
Peru	Перу	peru
Poland	Польша	polʲʃa
Portugal	Португалия	portugalija
Romania	Румыния	rumınija
Russia	Россия	rossija
Saudi Arabia	Сауд Аравиясы	saud aravijası
Scotland	Шотландия	ʃotlandija
Senegal	Сенегал	senegal
Serbia	Сербия	serbija
Slovakia	Словакия	slovakija
Slovenia	Словения	slovenija
South Africa	ТАР	tar
South Korea	Түштүк Корея	tyʃtyk koreja
Spain	Испания	ispanija
Suriname	Суринам	surinam
Sweden	Швеция	ʃvetsija
Switzerland	Швейцария	ʃvejtsarija
Syria	Сирия	sirija
Taiwan	Тайвань	tajvanʲ
Tajikistan	Тажикистан	tadʒikistan
Tanzania	Танзания	tanzanija
Tasmania	Тасмания	tasmanija
Thailand	Таиланд	tailand
Tunisia	Тунис	tunis
Turkey	Түркия	tyrkija
Turkmenistan	Туркмения	turkmenija
Ukraine	Украина	ukraina
United Arab Emirates	Бириккен Араб Эмираттары	birikken arab emirattarı
United States of America	Америка Кошмо Штаттары	amerika koʃmo ʃtattarı
Uruguay	Уругвай	urugvaj
Uzbekistan	Өзбекистан	øzbekistan
Vatican	Ватикан	vatikan
Venezuela	Венесуэла	venesuela
Vietnam	Вьетнам	vjetnam
Zanzibar	Занзибар	zanzibar

GASTRONOMIC GLOSSARY

This section contains a lot of
words and terms associated
with food. This dictionary will
make it easier for you to
understand the menu at a
restaurant and choose
the right dish

T&P Books Publishing

aftertaste	даамдануу	daamdanuu
almond	бадам	badam
anise	анис	anis
aperitif	аперитив	aperitiv
appetite	табит	tabit
appetizer	ысылык	ısılık
apple	алма	alma
apricot	өрүк	øryk
artichoke	артишок	artiʃok
asparagus	спаржа	spardʒa
Atlantic salmon	сёмга	sʲomga
avocado	авокадо	avokado
bacon	бекон	bekon
banana	банан	banan
barley	арпа	arpa
bartender	бармен	barmen
basil	райхон	rajχon
bay leaf	лавр жалбырагы	lavr dʒalbıragı
beans	буурчак	buurʧak
beef	уй эти	uj eti
beer	сыра	sıra
beet	кызылча	kızılʧa
bell pepper	таттуу перец	tattuu perets
berries	жер жемиштер	dʒer dʒemiʃter
berry	жер жемиш	dʒer dʒemiʃ
bilberry	кара моюл	kara mojʉl
birch bolete	подберёзовик	podberʲozovik
bitter	ачуу	aʧuu
black coffee	кара кофе	kara kofe
black pepper	кара мурч	kara murʧ
black tea	кара чай	kara ʧaj
blackberry	кара бүлдүркөн	kara byldyrkøn
blackcurrant	кара карагат	kara karagat
boiled	сууга бышырылган	suuga bıʃırılgan
bottle opener	ачкыч	aʧkıʧ
bread	нан	nan
breakfast	таңкы тамак	taŋkı tamak
bream	лещ	leʃʧ
broccoli	брокколи капустасы	brokkoli kapustası
Brussels sprouts	брюссель капустасы	brʉsselʲ kapustası
buckwheat	гречиха	gretʃiχa
butter	ак май	ak maj
buttercream	крем	krem
cabbage	капуста	kapusta

cake	пирожное	pirodʒnoe
cake	торт	tort
calorie	калория	kalorija
can opener	ачкыч	aʧkıʧ
candy	конфета	konfeta
canned food	консерва	konserva
cappuccino	капучино	kapuʧino
caraway	зира	zira
carbohydrates	көмүрсуулар	kømyrsuular
carbonated	газдалган	gazdalgan
carp	карп	karp
carrot	сабиз	sabiz
catfish	жаян	dʒajan
cauliflower	гүлдүү капуста	gyldyy kapusta
caviar	урук	uruk
celery	сельдерей	selʲderej
cep	ак козу карын	ak kozu karın
cereal crops	дан эгиндери	dan eginderi
champagne	шампан	ʃampan
chanterelle	лисичка	lisiʧka
check	эсеп	esep
cheese	сыр	sır
chewing gum	сагыз	sagız
chicken	тоок	took
chocolate	шоколад	ʃokolad
chocolate	шоколаддан	ʃokoladdan
cinnamon	корица	koritsa
clear soup	ынак сорпо	ınak sorpo
cloves	гвоздика	gvozdika
cocktail	коктейль	koktejlʲ
coconut	кокос жаңгагы	kokos dʒaŋgagı
cod	треска	treska
coffee	кофе	kofe
coffee with milk	сүттөлгөн кофе	syttølgøn kofe
cognac	коньяк	konjak
cold	муздак	muzdak
condensed milk	коютулган сүт	kojutulgan syt
condiment	татымал	tatımal
confectionery	кондитер азыктары	konditer azıktarı
cookies	печенье	peʧenje
coriander	кориандр	koriandr
corkscrew	штопор	ʃtopor
corn	жүгөрү	dʒygøry
corn	жүгөрү	dʒygøry
cornflakes	жарылган жүгөрү	dʒarılgan dʒygøry
course, dish	тамак	tamak
cowberry	брусника	brusnika
crab	краб	krab
cranberry	клюква	klʉkva
cream	каймак	kajmak
crumb	күкүм	kykym
crustaceans	рак сыяктуулар	rak sıjaktuular

cucumber	бадыраң	badıraŋ
cuisine	даам	daam
cup	чөйчөк	tʃøjtʃøk
dark beer	коңур сыра	koŋur sıra
date	курма	kurma
death cap	поганка	poganka
dessert	десерт	desert
diet	мүнөз тамак	mynøz tamak
dill	укроп	ukrop
dinner	кечки тамак	ketʃki tamak
dried	кургатылган	kurgatılgan
drinking water	ичүүчү суу	itʃyytʃy suu
duck	өрдөк	ørdøk
ear	машак	maʃak
edible mushroom	желе турган козу карын	dʒele turgan kozu karın
eel	угорь	ugorʲ
egg	жумуртка	dʒumurtka
egg white	жумуртканын агы	dʒumurtkanın agı
egg yolk	жумуртканын сарысы	dʒumurtkanın sarısı
eggplant	баклажан	bakladʒan
eggs	жумурткалар	dʒumurtkalar
Enjoy your meal!	Тамагыңыз таттуу болсун!	tamagıŋız tattuu bolsun!
fats	майлар	majlar
fig	анжир	andʒir
filling	начинка	natʃinka
fish	балык	balık
flatfish	камбала	kambala
flour	ун	un
fly agaric	мухомор	muχomor
food	тамак	tamak
fork	вилка	vilka
freshly squeezed juice	түз сыгылып алынган шире	tyz sıgılıp alıngan ʃire
fried	куурулган	kuurulgan
fried eggs	куурулган жумуртка	kuurulgan dʒumurtka
frozen	тоңдурулган	toŋdurulgan
fruit	мөмө	mømø
fruits	мөмө-жемиш	mømø-dʒemiʃ
game	илбээсин	ilbeesin
gammon	сан эт	san et
garlic	сарымсак	sarımsak
gin	джин	dʒin
ginger	имбирь	imbirʲ
glass	ыстакан	ıstakan
glass	бокал	bokal
goose	каз	kaz
gooseberry	крыжовник	krıdʒovnik
grain	дан	dan
grape	жүзүм	dʒyzym
grapefruit	грейпфрут	grejpfrut
green tea	жашыл чай	dʒaʃıl tʃaj

greens	көк чөп	køk ʧøp
groats	акшак	akʃak
halibut	палтус	paltus
ham	ветчина	vettʃina
hamburger	фарш	farʃ
hamburger	гамбургер	gamburger
hazelnut	токой жаңгагы	tokoj ʤaŋgagɪ
herring	сельдь	selʲdʲ
honey	бал	bal
horseradish	хрен	χren
hot	ысык	ɪsɪk
ice	муз	muz
ice-cream	бал муздак	bal muzdak
instant coffee	эрүүчү кофе	eryyʧy kofe
jam	джем, конфитюр	ʤem, konfitʉr
jam	кыям	kɪjam
juice	шире	ʃire
kidney bean	төө буурчак	tøø buurʧak
kiwi	киви	kivi
knife	бычак	bɪʧak
lamb	кой эти	koj eti
lemon	лимон	limon
lemonade	лимонад	limonad
lentil	жасмык	ʤasmɪk
lettuce	салат	salat
light beer	ачык сыра	aʧɪk sɪra
liqueur	ликёр	likʲor
liquors	спирт ичимдиктери	spirt iʧimdikteri
liver	боор	boor
lunch	түшкү тамак	tyʃky tamak
mackerel	скумбрия	skumbrija
mandarin	мандарин	mandarin
mango	манго	mango
margarine	маргарин	margarin
marmalade	мармелад	marmelad
mashed potatoes	эзилген картошка	ezilgen kartoʃka
mayonnaise	майонез	majonez
meat	эт	et
melon	коон	koon
menu	меню	menʉ
milk	сүт	syt
milkshake	сүт коктейли	syt koktejli
millet	таруу	taruu
mineral water	минерал суусу	mineral suusu
morel	сморчок	smorʧok
mushroom	козу карын	kozu karɪn
mustard	горчица	gorʧitsa
non-alcoholic	алкоголсуз	alkogolsuz
noodles	кесме	kesme
oats	сулу	sulu
olive oil	зайтун майы	zajtun majɪ
olives	зайтун	zajtun

omelet	омлет	omlet
onion	пияз	pijaz
orange	апельсин	apelʲsin
orange juice	апельсин ширеси	apelʲsin ʃiresi
orange-cap boletus	подосиновик	podosinovik
oyster	устрица	ustritsa
pâté	паштет	paʃtet
papaya	папайя	papaja
paprika	паприка	paprika
parsley	петрушка	petruʃka
pasta	макарон	makaron
pea	нокот	nokot
peach	шабдаалы	ʃabdaalı
peanut	арахис	araχis
pear	алмурут	almurut
peel	сырты	sırtı
perch	окунь	okunʲ
pickled	маринаддагы	marinaddagı
pie	пирог	pirog
piece	бөлүк	bөlyk
pike	чортон	tʃorton
pike perch	судак	sudak
pineapple	ананас	ananas
pistachios	мисте	miste
pizza	пицца	pitsa
plate	табак	tabak
plum	кара өрүк	kara øryk
poisonous mushroom	уулуу козу карын	uuluu kozu karın
pomegranate	анар	anar
pork	чочко эти	tʃotʃko eti
porridge	ботко	botko
portion	порция	portsija
potato	картошка	kartoʃka
proteins	белоктор	beloktor
pub, bar	бар	bar
pudding	пудинг	puding
pumpkin	ашкабак	aʃkabak
rabbit	коен	koen
radish	шалгам	ʃalgam
raisin	мейиз	mejiz
raspberry	дан куурай	dan kuuraj
recipe	тамак жасоо ыкмасы	tamak dʒasoo ıkması
red pepper	кызыл калемпир	kızıl kalempir
red wine	кызыл шарап	kızıl ʃarap
redcurrant	кызыл карагат	kızıl karagat
refreshing drink	суусундук	suusunduk
rice	күрүч	kyrytʃ
rum	ром	rom
russula	сыроежка	sıroedʒka
rye	кара буудай	kara buudaj
saffron	заапаран	zaaparan
salad	салат	salat

salmon	лосось	lososj
salt	туз	tuz
salty	туздуу	tuzduu
sandwich	бутерброд	buterbrod
sardine	сардина	sardina
sauce	соус	sous
saucer	табак	tabak
sausage	колбаса	kolbasa
seafood	деңиз азыктары	deŋiz azıktarı
sesame	кунжут	kundʒut
shark	акула	akula
shrimp	креветка	krevetka
side dish	гарнир	garnir
slice	кесим	kesim
smoked	ышталган	ıʃtalgan
soft drink	алкоголсуз ичимдик	alkogolsuz itʃimdik
soup	сорпо	sorpo
soup spoon	аш кашык	aʃ kaʃık
sour cherry	алча	altʃa
sour cream	сметана	smetana
soy	соя	soja
spaghetti	спагетти	spagetti
sparkling	газы менен	gazı menen
spice	татымал	tatımal
spinach	шпинат	ʃpinat
spiny lobster	лангуст	langust
spoon	кашык	kaʃık
squid	кальмар	kaljmar
steak	бифштекс	bifʃteks
still	газсыз	gazsız
strawberry	кулпунай	kulpunaj
sturgeon	осетрина	osetrina
sugar	кум шекер	kum-ʃeker
sunflower oil	күн карама майы	kyn karama majı
sweet	таттуу	tattuu
sweet cherry	гилас	gilas
taste, flavor	даам	daam
tasty	даамдуу	daamduu
tea	чай	tʃaj
teaspoon	чай кашык	tʃaj kaʃık
tip	чайпул	tʃajpul
tomato	помидор	pomidor
tomato juice	томат ширеси	tomat ʃiresi
tongue	тил	til
toothpick	тиш чукугуч	tiʃ tʃukugutʃ
trout	форель	forelj
tuna	тунец	tunets
turkey	күрп	kyrp
turnip	шалгам	ʃalgam
veal	торпок эти	torpok eti
vegetable oil	өсүмдүк майы	øsymdyk majı
vegetables	жашылча	dʒaʃiltʃa

vegetarian	эттен чанган	etten tʃangan
vegetarian	этсиз даярдалган	etsiz dajardalgan
vermouth	вермут	vermut
vienna sausage	сосиска	sosiska
vinegar	уксус	uksus
vitamin	витамин	vitamin
vodka	арак	arak
wafers	вафли	vafli
waiter	официант	ofitsiant
waitress	официант кыз	ofitsiant kız
walnut	жаңгак	dʒaŋgak
water	суу	suu
watermelon	арбуз	arbuz
wheat	буудай	buudaj
whiskey	виски	viski
white wine	ак шарап	ak ʃarap
wild strawberry	кызылгат	kızılgat
wine	шарап	ʃarap
wine list	шарап картасы	ʃarap kartası
with ice	музу менен	muzu menen
yogurt	йогурт	jogurt
zucchini	кабачок	kabatʃok

Kyrgyz-English gastronomic glossary

өрүк	øryk	apricot
өрдөк	ørdøk	duck
өсүмдүк майы	øsymdyk majı	vegetable oil
авокадо	avokado	avocado
ак козу карын	ak kozu karın	cep
ак май	ak maj	butter
ак шарап	ak ʃarap	white wine
акула	akula	shark
акшак	akʃak	groats
алкоголсуз	alkogolsuz	non-alcoholic
алкоголсуз ичимдик	alkogolsuz itʃimdik	soft drink
алма	alma	apple
алмурут	almurut	pear
алча	altʃa	sour cherry
ананас	ananas	pineapple
анар	anar	pomegranate
анжир	andʒir	fig
анис	anis	anise
апельсин	apelʲsin	orange
апельсин ширеси	apelʲsin ʃiresi	orange juice
аперитив	aperitiv	aperitif
арак	arak	vodka
арахис	araχis	peanut
арбуз	arbuz	watermelon
арпа	arpa	barley
артишок	artiʃok	artichoke
ачкыч	atʃkıtʃ	bottle opener
ачкыч	atʃkıtʃ	can opener
ачуу	atʃuu	bitter
ачык сыра	atʃık sıra	light beer
аш кашык	aʃ kaʃık	soup spoon
ашкабак	aʃkabak	pumpkin
бөлүк	bølyk	piece
бадам	badam	almond
бадыраң	badıraŋ	cucumber
баклажан	bakladʒan	eggplant
бал	bal	honey
бал муздак	bal muzdak	ice-cream
балык	balık	fish
банан	banan	banana
бар	bar	pub, bar
бармен	barmen	bartender
бекон	bekon	bacon
белоктор	beloktor	proteins

бифштекс	bifʃteks	steak
бокал	bokal	glass
боор	boor	liver
ботко	botko	porridge
брокколи капустасы	brokkoli kapustası	broccoli
брусника	brusnika	cowberry
брюссель капустасы	brᵾsselⁱ kapustası	Brussels sprouts
бутерброд	buterbrod	sandwich
буудай	buudaj	wheat
буурчак	buurtʃak	beans
бычак	bıtʃak	knife
вафли	vafli	wafers
вермут	vermut	vermouth
ветчина	vettʃina	ham
вилка	vilka	fork
виски	viski	whiskey
витамин	vitamin	vitamin
гүлдүү капуста	gyldyy kapusta	cauliflower
газдалган	gazdalgan	carbonated
газсыз	gazsız	still
газы менен	gazı menen	sparkling
гамбургер	gamburger	hamburger
гарнир	garnir	side dish
гвоздика	gvozdika	cloves
гилас	gilas	sweet cherry
горчица	gortʃitsa	mustard
грейпфрут	grejpfrut	grapefruit
гречиха	gretʃıχa	buckwheat
даам	daam	cuisine
даам	daam	taste, flavor
даамдануу	daamdanuu	aftertaste
даамдуу	daamduu	tasty
дан	dan	grain
дан куурай	dan kuuraj	raspberry
дан эгиндери	dan eginderi	cereal crops
деңиз азыктары	deŋiz azıktarı	seafood
десерт	desert	dessert
джем, конфитюр	dʒem, konfitᵾr	jam
джин	dʒin	gin
жүгөрү	dʒygøry	corn
жүгөрү	dʒygøry	corn
жүзүм	dʒyzym	grape
жаңгак	dʒaŋgak	walnut
жарылган жүгөрү	dʒarılgan dʒygøry	cornflakes
жасмык	dʒasmık	lentil
жашыл чай	dʒaʃıl tʃaj	green tea
жашылча	dʒaʃıltʃa	vegetables
жаян	dʒajan	catfish
желе турган козу карын	dʒele turgan kozu karın	edible mushroom
жер жемиш	dʒer dʒemiʃ	berry
жер жемиштер	dʒer dʒemiʃter	berries
жумуртка	dʒumurtka	egg

жумурткалар	ʤumurtkalar	eggs
жумуртканын агы	ʤumurtkanın agı	egg white
жумуртканын сарысы	ʤumurtkanın sarısı	egg yolk
заапаран	zaaparan	saffron
зайтун	zajtun	olives
зайтун майы	zajtun majı	olive oil
зира	zira	caraway
илбээсин	ilbeesin	game
имбирь	imbirʲ	ginger
ичүүчү суу	iʧyyʧy suu	drinking water
йогурт	jogurt	yogurt
күкүм	kykym	crumb
күн карама майы	kyn karama majı	sunflower oil
күрүч	kyryʧ	rice
күрп	kyrp	turkey
көк чөп	køk ʧøp	greens
көмүрсуулар	kømyrsuular	carbohydrates
кабачок	kabaʧok	zucchini
каз	kaz	goose
каймак	kajmak	cream
калория	kalorija	calorie
кальмар	kalʲmar	squid
камбала	kambala	flatfish
капуста	kapusta	cabbage
капучино	kapuʧino	cappuccino
кара өрүк	kara øryk	plum
кара булдүркөн	kara byldyrkøn	blackberry
кара буудай	kara buudaj	rye
кара карагат	kara karagat	blackcurrant
кара кофе	kara kofe	black coffee
кара моюл	kara mojʉl	bilberry
кара мурч	kara murʧ	black pepper
кара чай	kara ʧaj	black tea
карп	karp	carp
картошка	kartoʃka	potato
кашык	kaʃık	spoon
кесим	kesim	slice
кесме	kesme	noodles
кечки тамак	keʧki tamak	dinner
киви	kivi	kiwi
клюква	klʉkva	cranberry
коңур сыра	koŋur sıra	dark beer
коен	koen	rabbit
козу карын	kozu karın	mushroom
кой эти	koj eti	lamb
кокос жаңгагы	kokos ʤaŋgagı	coconut
коктейль	koktejlʲ	cocktail
колбаса	kolbasa	sausage
кондитер азыктары	konditer azıktarı	confectionery
консерва	konserva	canned food
конфета	konfeta	candy
коньяк	konjak	cognac

коон	koon	melon
кориандр	koriandr	coriander
корица	koriʦa	cinnamon
кофе	kofe	coffee
коютулган сүт	kojʉtulgan syt	condensed milk
краб	krab	crab
креветка	krevetka	shrimp
крем	krem	buttercream
крыжовник	krıʤovnik	gooseberry
кулпунай	kulpunaj	strawberry
кум шекер	kum-ʃeker	sugar
кунжут	kunʤut	sesame
кургатылган	kurgatılgan	dried
курма	kurma	date
куурулган	kuurulgan	fried
куурулган жумуртка	kuurulgan ʤumurtka	fried eggs
кызыл калемпир	kızıl kalempir	red pepper
кызыл карагат	kızıl karagat	redcurrant
кызыл шарап	kızıl ʃarap	red wine
кызылгат	kızılgat	wild strawberry
кызылча	kızılʧa	beet
кыям	kıjam	jam
лавр жалбырагы	lavr ʤalbıragı	bay leaf
лангуст	langust	spiny lobster
лещ	leʃʧ	bream
ликёр	likʲor	liqueur
лимон	limon	lemon
лимонад	limonad	lemonade
лисичка	lisiʧka	chanterelle
лосось	lososʲ	salmon
мүнөз тамак	mynøz tamak	diet
мөмө	mømø	fruit
мөмө-жемиш	mømø-ʤemiʃ	fruits
майлар	majlar	fats
майонез	majonez	mayonnaise
макарон	makaron	pasta
манго	mango	mango
мандарин	mandarin	mandarin
маргарин	margarin	margarine
маринаддагы	marinaddagı	pickled
мармелад	marmelad	marmalade
машак	maʃak	ear
мейиз	mejiz	raisin
меню	menʉ	menu
минерал суусу	mineral suusu	mineral water
мисте	miste	pistachios
муз	muz	ice
муздак	muzdak	cold
музу менен	muzu menen	with ice
мухомор	muχomor	fly agaric
нан	nan	bread
начинка	natʃinka	filling

нокот	nokot	pea
окунь	okunʲ	perch
омлет	omlet	omelet
осетрина	osetrina	sturgeon
официант	ofitsiant	waiter
официант кыз	ofitsiant kız	waitress
палтус	paltus	halibut
папайя	papaja	papaya
паприка	paprika	paprika
паштет	paʃtet	pâté
петрушка	petruʃka	parsley
печенье	petʃenje	cookies
пирог	pirog	pie
пирожное	pirodʒnoe	cake
пицца	pitsa	pizza
пияз	pijaz	onion
поганка	poganka	death cap
подберёзовик	podberʲozovik	birch bolete
подосиновик	podosinovik	orange-cap boletus
помидор	pomidor	tomato
порция	portsija	portion
пудинг	puding	pudding
райхон	rajxon	basil
рак сыяктуулар	rak sıjaktuular	crustaceans
ром	rom	rum
сүт	syt	milk
сүт коктейли	syt koktejli	milkshake
сүттөлгөн кофе	syttølgøn kofe	coffee with milk
сабиз	sabiz	carrot
сагыз	sagız	chewing gum
салат	salat	lettuce
салат	salat	salad
сан эт	san et	gammon
сардина	sardina	sardine
сарымсак	sarımsak	garlic
сельдерей	selʲderej	celery
сельдь	selʲdʲ	herring
сёмга	sʲomga	Atlantic salmon
скумбрия	skumbrija	mackerel
сметана	smetana	sour cream
сморчок	smortʃok	morel
сорпо	sorpo	soup
сосиска	sosiska	vienna sausage
соус	sous	sauce
соя	soja	soy
спагетти	spagetti	spaghetti
спаржа	spardʒa	asparagus
спирт ичимдиктери	spirt itʃimdikteri	liquors
судак	sudak	pike perch
сулу	sulu	oats
суу	suu	water
сууга бышырылган	suuga bıʃırılgan	boiled

суусундук	suusunduk	refreshing drink
сыр	sır	cheese
сыра	sıra	beer
сыроежка	sıroedʒka	russula
сырты	sırtı	peel
түз сыгылып алынган шире	tyz sıgılıp alıngan ʃire	freshly squeezed juice
түшкү тамак	tyʃky tamak	lunch
төө буурчак	tøø buurtʃak	kidney bean
таңкы тамак	taŋkı tamak	breakfast
табак	tabak	saucer
табак	tabak	plate
табит	tabit	appetite
Тамагыңыз таттуу болсун!	tamagıŋız tattuu bolsun!	Enjoy your meal!
тамак	tamak	course, dish
тамак	tamak	food
тамак жасоо ыкмасы	tamak dʒasoo ıkması	recipe
таруу	taruu	millet
таттуу	tattuu	sweet
таттуу перец	tattuu perets	bell pepper
татымал	tatımal	condiment
татымал	tatımal	spice
тил	til	tongue
тиш чукугуч	tiʃ tʃukugutʃ	toothpick
тоңдурулган	toŋdurulgan	frozen
токой жаңгагы	tokoj dʒaŋgagı	hazelnut
томат ширеси	tomat ʃiresi	tomato juice
тоок	took	chicken
торпок эти	torpok eti	veal
торт	tort	cake
треска	treska	cod
туз	tuz	salt
туздуу	tuzduu	salty
тунец	tunets	tuna
угорь	ugorʲ	eel
уй эти	uj eti	beef
укроп	ukrop	dill
уксус	uksus	vinegar
ун	un	flour
урук	uruk	caviar
устрица	ustritsa	oyster
уулуу козу карын	uuluu kozu karın	poisonous mushroom
фарш	farʃ	hamburger
форель	forelʲ	trout
хрен	χren	horseradish
чөйчөк	tʃøjtʃøk	cup
чай	tʃaj	tea
чай кашык	tʃaj kaʃık	teaspoon
чайпул	tʃajpul	tip
чортон	tʃorton	pike
чочко эти	tʃotʃko eti	pork

шабдаалы	ʃabdaalı	peach
шалгам	ʃalgam	turnip
шалгам	ʃalgam	radish
шампан	ʃampan	champagne
шарап	ʃarap	wine
шарап картасы	ʃarap kartası	wine list
шире	ʃire	juice
шоколад	ʃokolad	chocolate
шоколаддан	ʃokoladdan	chocolate
шпинат	ʃpinat	spinach
штопор	ʃtopor	corkscrew
ынак сорпо	ınak sorpo	clear soup
ыстакан	ıstakan	glass
ысык	ısık	hot
ысылык	ısılık	appetizer
ышталган	ıʃtalgan	smoked
эзилген картошка	ezilgen kartoʃka	mashed potatoes
эрүүчү кофе	eryytʃy kofe	instant coffee
эсеп	esep	check
эт	et	meat
этсиз даярдалган	etsiz dajardalgan	vegetarian
эттен чанган	etten tʃangan	vegetarian